AAT

Qualifications and Credit Framework (QCF)
AQ2013
LEVEL 4 DIPLOMA IN ACCOUNTING

WORKBOOK

Internal Control and
Accounting Systems

2015 Edition

For assessments from September 2015

Third edition June 2015
ISBN 9781 4727 2215 7

Previous edition
ISBN 9781 4727 0949 3

British Library Cataloguing-in-Publication Data
A catalogue record for this book is available from the British
Library

Published by
BPP Learning Media Ltd
BPP House
Aldine Place
London
W12 8AA

www.bpp.com/learningmedia

Printed in the United Kingdom by Martins of Berwick
Sea View Works
Spittal
Berwick-Upon-Tweed
TD15 1RS

BPP
LEARNING MEDIA

CONTENTS

BPP LEARNING MEDIA'S AAT MATERIALS

The AAT's assessments fall within the **Qualifications and Credit Framework** and most papers are assessed by way of an on demand **computer based assessment**. BPP Learning Media has invested heavily to ensure our materials are as relevant as possible for this method of assessment. In particular, our **suite of online resources** ensures that you are prepared for online testing by allowing you to practise numerous online tasks that are similar to the tasks you will encounter in the AAT's assessments.

Resources

The BPP range of resources comprises:

- **Texts**, covering all the knowledge and understanding needed by students, with numerous illustrations of 'how it works', practical examples and tasks for you to use to consolidate your learning. The majority of tasks within the texts have been written in an interactive style that reflects the style of the online tasks we anticipate the AAT will set. When you purchase a Text you are also granted free access to your Text content online.

- **Question Banks**, including additional learning questions plus the AAT's sample assessment(s) and a number of BPP full practice assessments. Full answers to all questions and assessments, prepared by BPP Learning Media Ltd, are included. Our question banks are provided free of charge online.

- **Passcards**, which are handy pocket-sized revision tools designed to fit in a handbag or briefcase to enable you to revise anywhere at anytime. All major points are covered in the Passcards which have been designed to assist you in consolidating knowledge.

- **Workbooks**, which have been designed to cover the units that are assessed by way of computer based project/case study. The workbooks contain many practical tasks to assist in the learning process and also a sample assessment or project to work through.

- **Lecturers' resources**, for units assessed by computer based assessments. These provide a further bank of tasks, answers and full practice assessments for classroom use, available separately only to lecturers whose colleges adopt BPP Learning Media material.

This Workbook for Internal Control and Accounting Systems has been written specifically to ensure comprehensive yet concise coverage of the AAT's **AQ2013** learning outcomes and assessment criteria.

Each chapter contains:

- Clear, step by step explanation of the topic
- Logical progression and linking from one chapter to the next
- Numerous illustrations of 'how it works'
- Interactive tasks within the text of the chapter itself, with answers at the back of the book
- Test your learning questions of varying complexity, again with answers supplied at the back of the book

The emphasis in all tasks and test questions is on the practical application of the skills acquired.

Supplements

From time to time we may need to publish supplementary materials to one of our titles. This can be for a variety of reasons, from a small change in the AAT unit guidance to new legislation coming into effect between editions.

You should check our supplements page regularly for anything that may affect your learning materials. All supplements are available free of charge on our supplements page on our website at:

www.bpp.com/about-bpp/aboutBPP/StudentInfo#q4

Customer feedback

If you have any comments about this book, please email nisarahmed@bpp.com or write to Nisar Ahmed, AAT Head of Programme, BPP Learning Media Ltd, BPP House, Aldine Place, London W12 8AA.

Any feedback we receive is taken into consideration when we periodically update our materials, including comments on style, depth and coverage of AAT standards.

In addition, although our products pass through strict technical checking and quality control processes, unfortunately errors may occasionally slip through when producing material to tight deadlines.

When we learn of an error in a batch of our printed materials, either from internal review processes or from customers using our materials, we want to make sure customers are made aware of this as soon as possible and the appropriate action is taken to minimise the impact on student learning.

BPP LEARNING MEDIA

As a result, when we become aware of any such errors we will:

1) Include details of the error and, if necessary, PDF prints of any revised pages under the related subject heading on our 'supplements' page at: www.bpp.com/about-bpp/aboutBPP/StudentInfo#q4

2) Update the source files ahead of any further printing of the materials

3) Investigate the reason for the error and take appropriate action to minimise the risk of reoccurrence

A NOTE ON TERMINOLOGY

The AAT AQ2013 standards and assessments use international terminology based on International Financial Reporting Standards (IFRSs). Although you may be familiar with UK terminology, you need to now know the equivalent international terminology for your assessments.

The following information is taken from an article on the AAT's website and compares IFRS terminology with UK GAAP terminology. It then goes on to describe the impact of IFRS terminology on students studying for each level of the AAT QCF qualification.

Note that since the article containing the information below was published, there have been changes made to some IFRSs. Therefore BPP Learning Media have updated the table and other information below to reflect these changes.

In particular, the primary performance statement under IFRSs which was formerly known as the 'income statement' or the 'statement of comprehensive income' is now called the 'statement of profit or loss' or the 'statement of profit or loss and other comprehensive income'.

What is the impact of IFRS terms on AAT assessments?

The list shown in the table that follows gives the 'translation' between UK GAAP and IFRS.

UK GAAP	IFRS
Final accounts	Financial statements
Trading and profit and loss account	**Statement of profit or loss (or statement of profit or loss and other comprehensive income)**
Turnover or Sales	Revenue or Sales Revenue
Sundry income	Other operating income
Interest payable	Finance costs
Sundry expenses	Other operating costs
Operating profit	Profit from operations
Net profit/loss	Profit/loss for the year/period

UK GAAP	IFRS
Balance sheet	**Statement of financial position**
Fixed assets	Non-current assets
Net book value	Carrying amount
Tangible assets	Property, plant and equipment
Reducing balance depreciation	Diminishing balance depreciation
Depreciation/Depreciation expense(s)	Depreciation charge(s)
Stocks	Inventories
Trade debtors or Debtors	Trade receivables
Prepayments	Other receivables
Debtors and prepayments	Trade and other receivables
Cash at bank and in hand	Cash and cash equivalents
Trade creditors or Creditors	Trade payables
Accruals	Other payables
Creditors and accruals	Trade and other payables
Long-term liabilities	Non-current liabilities
Capital and reserves	Equity (limited companies)
Profit and loss balance	Retained earnings
Minority interest	Non-controlling interest
Cash flow statement	**Statement of cash flows**

This is certainly not a comprehensive list, which would run to several pages, but it does cover the main terms that you will come across in your studies and assessments. However, you won't need to know all of these In the early stages of your studies – some of the terms will not be used until you reach Level 4. For each level of the AAT qualification, the points to bear in mind are as follows:

Level 2 Certificate in Accounting

The IFRS terms do not impact greatly at this level. Make sure you are familiar with 'receivables' (also referred to as 'trade receivables'), 'payables' (also referred to as 'trade payables'), and 'inventories'. The terms sales ledger and purchases ledger – together with their control accounts – will continue to be used. Sometimes the control accounts might be called 'trade receivables control account' and 'trade payables control account'. The other term to be aware of is 'non-current asset' – this may be used in some assessments.

Level 3 Diploma in Accounting

At this level you need to be familiar with the term 'financial statements'. The financial statements comprise a 'statement of profit or loss' (previously known as an income statement), and a 'statement of financial position'. In the statement of profit or loss the term 'revenue' or 'sales revenue' takes the place of 'sales', and 'profit for the year' replaces 'net profit'. Other terms may be used in the statement of financial position – eg 'non-current assets' and 'carrying amount'. However, specialist limited company terms are not required at this level.

Level 4 Diploma in Accounting

At Level 4 a wider range of IFRS terms is needed, and in the case of Financial statements, are already in use – particularly those relating to limited companies. Note especially that a statement of profit or loss becomes a 'statement of profit or loss and other comprehensive income'.

Note: The information above was taken from an AAT article from the 'assessment news' area of the AAT website (www.aat.org.uk). However, it has been adapted by BPP Learning Media for changes in international terminology since the article was published and for any changes needed to reflect the move from AQ2010 to AQ2013.

STANDARDS OF COMPETENCE

LEARNING OUTCOMES OF ISYS

This paper is made up of one units under the new Qualifications and Curriculum Framework (QCF).

One purpose of this unit is to ensure that learners know and understand the role of accounting in an organisation, and why internal controls should be in place.

Another is to ensure that learners are able to communicate clearly in writing, at a level 4 standard and in a manner appropriate to the workplace.

The unit aims to ensure that learners understand the principles of internal control. It has set learning outcomes so that learners are able to identify the role of accounting in general, and internal controls specifically, within an organisation. They must be able to make informed reasoned judgements to inform management on how to implement or improve systems within an organisation.

The unit also aims to ensure that learners can evaluate accounting systems within an organisation and consider whether they are appropriate to that organisation or not. They should be able to identify the organisation's accounting system requirements, carry out ethical and sustainability evaluations of the accounting systems, explain where improvements could be made and make valid suggestions about how to do this through communicating their recommendations to management in a clear manner, supported by reasoned argument. They should also be able to identify the impact that changes would have on the system and its users.

The learning outcomes of the unit are:

- Understand the role of accounting within an organisation
- Understand the importance and use of internal control systems
- Evaluate the accounting system and identify areas for improvement
- Conduct an ethical evaluation of the accounting systems
- Conduct a sustainability evaluation of the accounting system
- Make recommendations to improve the accounting system

Each of the learning outcomes above has a number of assessment criteria attached to it, that learners will need to demonstrate competence in to complete this paper.

The AAT have also published, in unit guides, set guidance on the requirements of each of the assessment criteria.

Introduction

Each chapter in this companion is mapped to the learning outcomes and assessment criteria below.

Principles of Internal Control and Evaluating Accounting Systems

Paper Commentary

This paper is about your ability to review accounting systems, and their appropriateness to a chosen organisation, including the internal controls in place.

Learning Outcomes contained within this unit are:

- Understand the role of accounting within an organisation
- Understand the importance and use of internal control systems
- Evaluate the accounting system and identify areas for improvement
- Conduct an ethical evaluation of the accounting systems
- Conduct a sustainability evaluation of the accounting system
- Make recommendations to improve the accounting system

BPP
LEARNING MEDIA

Assessment Criteria

Learning Outcome	Assessment Criteria	Chapter(s)
1. Understand the role of accounting within the organisation	1.1 Describe the purpose, structure and organisation of the accounting function and its relationships with other functions within the organisation	3
	1.2 Explain the various business purposes for which the following financial information is required: ■ Statement of profit or loss ■ Statement of cash flows ■ Statement of financial position	3
	1.3 Give an overview of the organisation's business and its critical external relationships with stakeholders	2
	1.4 Explain how the accounting systems are affected by the organisational structure, systems, procedures, and business transactions	3, 4
	1.5 Explain the effect on users of changes to accounting systems caused by: ■ External regulations ■ Organisational policies and procedures	2

Learning Outcome	Assessment Criteria	Chapter(s)
2. Understand the importance and use of internal control systems	2.1 Identify the external regulations that affect accounting practice	2
	2.2 Describe the causes of, and common types of, fraud and the impact of this on the organisation	6
	2.3 Explain methods that can be used to detect fraud within an accounting system	5, 6
	2.4 Explain the types of controls that can be put in place to ensure compliance with statutory or organisational requirements	5, 6
	2.5 Explain how an internal control system can support the accounting function	4, 5
3. Evaluate the accounting system and identify areas for improvement	3.1 Identify an organisation's accounting system requirements including hardware and software packages	3, 7
	3.2 Review record keeping systems to confirm whether they meet an organisation's requirements	4
	3.3 Identify weaknesses in and the potential for improvements to, the accounting system and consider their impact on the operation of the organisation	4
	3.4 Identify potential areas of fraud arising from lack of control within the accounting system and evaluate the risk	6

Learning Outcome	Assessment Criteria	Chapter(s)
3. Evaluate the accounting system and identify areas for improvement	3.5 Review methods of operating for cost effectiveness, reliability and speed	4, 7
4. Conduct an ethical evaluation of the accounting systems	4.1 Evaluate the accounting system against ethical principles	4
	4.2 Identify actual or possible breaches of ethics	4
5. Conduct a sustainability evaluation of the accounting system	5.1 Evaluate the accounting system against sustainable principles	4
	5.2 Identify where improvements could be made to improve sustainability	4
6. Make recommendations to improve the accounting system	6.1 Make recommendations for changes to the accounting system, including ethical and sustainability considerations, with a clear rationale and an explanation of any assumptions made	7
	6.2 Identify the effects that any recommended changes would have on the users of the system	4, 6 & 7
	6.3 Enable individuals to understand how to use an accounting system by the use of: ■ Training ■ Manuals ■ Written information ■ Help menus	4, 6 & 7
	6.4 Identify the implications of recommended changes in terms of time, financial costs, benefits, and operating procedures	7

ASSESSMENT STRATEGY

The assessment will take the form of a formal report written by the learner and assessed locally by the training provider. The report can be based upon the workplace of the student, or upon a scenario provided by AAT through SecureAssess as a computer-based project (CBP).

The report must be typed, completed and submitted for formal assessment within **four** months. The learner may, at the discretion of the assessor, then make a maximum of four further submissions. These must be submitted within two months of the initial report deadline, giving a total maximum assessment duration of **six** months.

The project takes the form of a report to management that analyses the accounting system within the organisation, assessing whether it is appropriate. It should specifically address the appropriateness of internal controls and make recommendations to improve both the system itself and the controls within it. In producing this report students will need to prove competence in their ability to review an organisation and its accounting systems, and an understanding of internal controls for different organisation types.

The report should be approximately 4,000 to 5,000 words long and should provide good analysis and an in depth review of one part of the accounting system of an organisation. It must cover all the assessment criteria.

The AAT has provided the following guidance on the required presentation and content of the report. We are grateful to the AAT for permitting us to reproduce this.

The report should be **presented** as follows:

- Written in the third person, that is to say not using any personal pronouns (for example: I, me, he or she).

- Spelling and grammar of a suitable level for a business report at Level 4, which is degree level standard.

- Word processed.

- The report must be numbered by section and paragraph number and mapped to the assessment.

- The report should show a 'reasonable' level of literacy skills. Whilst it would be unfair to penalise a candidate with a not yet competent decision for one spelling mistake, or the occasional use of a personal pronoun, overall the report should be fit for publication to the management of a company.

- The report should be split into sections, and these should be numbered. The paragraphs within each section should then be numbered (eg in section one, the first paragraph will be 1.1, then 1.2, 1.3 and onwards – section two will then start with 2.1, then 2.2 and so on.

The report should be mapped to the assessment criteria using the paragraph numbers for ease of assessment.

The report should be split into sections, and an example is given below. The sections can be:

- Terms of Reference

  The reasons why the report is being written, clearly identifying the scope of the report.

- Executive/management summary

  A short overview of the report's findings and the benefits that the organisation will gain by following the recommendations within the report.

- Introduction

  An overview of the accounting section under review, and how it relates to the rest of the organisation. This should detail critical internal and external stakeholders and any relevant external regulations. This should not be a history of the organisation, but used to give a context to the accounting system under review.

- Review of current accounting systems

  Depending on the type of organisation under review this may be a full accounting department which covers all aspects of the accounting functions within an organisation, or just one department within an accounts section - for example payroll.

The review should specifically cover the following areas:

- Record keeping systems - the purpose of financial reports, and the suitability of the organisation's current reports to meet organisational needs.

- Internal systems of control – identify how internal control supports the accounting system, the types of internal control in place and any controls that are missing.

- Fraud – causes of fraud, common types of fraud, methods used to detect fraud and potential areas for fraud within the organisation.

- Working methods/practices – including the use of appropriate computer software, hardware and the operating methods in terms of reliability, speed and cost effectiveness.

- Training – identify how training is or can be used to support staff.

- Professional ethics – identify any actual or likely breaches against AAT code.

- Sustainability – how the organisation takes responsibility for its own actions, and how it could make improvements against the principles of sustainability.

  - Weaknesses

    An analysis of the above, identifying weaknesses or areas where improvement could be made. Each weakness should be analysed and explained in depth, including the effect it has upon the organisation and/or staff.

    This can be written as a section focussing only on weaknesses then followed by a section on recommendations, or it may be written as both 'weaknesses and recommendations' with every weakness identified being followed by a recommendation; before the next weakness is explained.

  - Recommendations for improvement.

    For every weakness that has been identified there should be a recommendation made to attempt to improve the situation. This should include recommendations for both ethical and sustainability issues If the weaknesses have been written as a group then the recommendations should be written in the same order – for example weakness one should match the first recommendation made. The recommendations should concentrate on the effect that the changes would have both on the organisation, including corporate governance and sustainability and on individual members of staff. They may also highlight training needs or aids to improve staff performance and ethical issues.

  - Cost benefit analysis

    At least one of the recommendations made should be subject to a cost benefit analysis.

    It is not sufficient to say 'a large amount of money will be saved' or 'there are no costs associated with this recommendation as it is only staff time used'. Financial figures must be placed in the report, even if they are 'guesstimates'. Learners should be encouraged to use assumptions, and these should be accepted as long as they are realistic.

    Whilst not all benefits are quantifiable all costs are – and students should make any necessary assumptions or 'guesstimates' to allocate costs to such items as time, unknown salaries, or any other unknown expense involved in the recommended changes. All benefits should be identified, included those that cannot be allocated a financial figure. This can include such things as improved customer relationships, improved documentation systems or staff morale (though this could be allocated a financial benefit as improving staff turnover cuts recruitment costs).

–   Appendices

Any charts and diagrams or supporting evidence should be included here and cross -referenced within the text. Any appendices included should be referred to in the main body of the report – or in the case of supporting statements to cover missing assessment criteria, mapped and cross -referenced to a copy of the unit standards.

The assessment material (CBP) will be delivered online and assessed locally. The local assessor (training provider) will be required to ensure that all assessment criteria are covered. Learners will be required to demonstrate competence across the assessment criteria for this learning and assessment area.

The AAT also set out the following respective responsibilities of the learner and the assessor in their guidance on writing the report.

Responsibilities as a learner:

- Identify the theme for your report
- Meet with the assessor at agreed times
- Draft the report
- Map to the assessment criteria
- Present the final report
- Keep your assessor informed on progress
- Stick to target dates and deadlines

Responsibilities as an assessor:

- Schedule the assessment
- Agree the theme of the report
- Give guidance on the draft report
- Give additional assessment opportunities as necessary
- Assess the final report
- Hold an assessment interview if necessary

Duration of assessment

Note: The following information is taken from the AAT guidance for ICAS provided by the AAT at the date of publishing (June 2013).

The amount of teaching input will of course vary between training providers, but it is expected that once teaching has been completed, the report will be written and completed as follows.

AAT assessment

- For the first submission, learners must submit a substantial report for formal assessment within four months* of the scheduled assessment start date.

- After reviewing the leaner's first submission (substantial report) the assessor may permit the learner up to four further opportunities to submit additional supporting evidence. Additional submissions of evidence should be complete within six months* of the scheduled assessment start date or at the discretion of the assessor.

* For learners with reasonable adjustment and special consideration (RASC) please view the AAT RASC policy available online.

Workplace evidence and recognition of prior learning

Deadline setting for workplace evidence and recognition of prior learning is at the discretion of the assessor. A maximum of five submissions are allowed.

The role of accounting within the organisation

Learners should be able to give an overview of an organisation (real work place or scenario based) – identifying the important external relationships it has. This may include – but is not restricted to – any of the following: customers, suppliers, shareholders, banks, trade organisations, government departments/organisations. These will depend on the type of organisation that is being reviewed.

They should also be able to identify the relationship between other internal departments and the accounting function, and clearly define the structure, purpose and organisation of the accounting function within the overall organisation. They should know the reasons why financial reports are produced.

Learners need the skills to be able to determine what an organisation requires from its accounting systems. These requirements will differ depending on the nature and size of the organisation, and learners should be able to identify the requirements and benefits of different accounting systems/software/hardware packages to a specific organisation.

Evaluate the accounting system and identify areas for improvement

They will then need to review the accounting systems to ensure they meet these requirements. This can be achieved by identifying the strengths and weaknesses of the accounting system (not the organisation). This should include a review of the procedures used within the accounting system to ensure that the optimum results are being achieved especially in terms of time, financial costs, benefits and effectiveness. Learners should also identify external regulations that will influence the organisation's accounting practices, for example, accounting standards.

An accounting system may cover all accounting functions including, but not restricted to, accounts receivable, accounts payable, cash book and the general ledger, credit control, banking, payroll, petty cash, budgeting and management reporting. All of these may be evaluated in a small organisation with a simple structure, or just one or two areas may be evaluated in a larger, more complex, organisation.

The importance and use of internal control systems

The internal control system should be reviewed and evaluated for areas where there is a potential for errors and also for any possible areas of fraud. Areas where there is a potential for fraud should be highlighted and the risk should be graded.

Potential areas of fraud can include anything that poses a threat of loss to an organisation. Types of loss may include, but are not restricted to, monetary based, inventory based or time based frauds. Examples include fictitious employees or fictitious trade receivables being paid; over-ordering and theft of inventory; or employees who overstate the time they have worked. Risk of fraud can be graded as low, medium or high – or given numerical grades of 1 – 5 where the more serious the risk the higher the grade.

Learners should be aware of the common types of fraud, how these can be caused, and the impact that fraud has upon an organisation. They should be able to identify ways of detecting fraud and the types of internal controls that could be established to prevent these instances occurring. Other internal control mechanisms that are needed may also be identified to meet organisational **or** statutory requirements (Note – not necessarily both).

Conduct an ethical evaluation of the accounting systems

There should be an evaluation of the accounting system against the professional ethics of AAT and the organisation. Students should be able to identify actual or possible breaches of any of the five fundamental principles of the code of professional ethics. . Examples of this could include breaches of confidentiality, integrity, professional behaviour, objectivity and professional competence.

Conduct a sustainability evaluation of the accounting system

There should also be an evaluation of sustainability with the accounting system, and learners should be able to identify where improvements could be made. This should look at the impact that the organisation has on the environment, the economy or society. Examples of this could be to reduce the carbon footprint, reduce the use of natural resources (paper, electricity, petrol etc) or improving corporate social responsibility.

Learners will then need to review the weaknesses they have identified and explain their impact upon the organisation. This should be considered in terms of time, money and reputation (ie loss of revenue, time wasting, customer expectations not being met.)

Make recommendations to improve the accounting system

Learners will need to make clear and sensible recommendations to improve the weaknesses identified in the evaluation of the accounting systems. For every weakness identified there must be at least one recommendation made for improvement. The recommendations should include improving the areas of professional ethics, and sustainability within the organisation.

If a learner has identified just one weakness within a system then they should compare two or three possible remedial options and identify which they feel is the best solution, with justification of their recommendation.

For example a learner working in an accountant's office may identify a weakness as being a client still using a manual system for their accounting records. Their recommendation may be to computerise the system. However, the learner should then review the possible options – choosing between a spreadsheet package (for example, Excel); a computerised accounting package (for example, Sage, Tass Books); or opting for a tailor made system (for example Innsite). They should then compare the advantages and disadvantages of each option before making the decision as to which best suits the needs of the organisation. This could include the amount of sustainable resources that each system would use.

If, however, the learner has identified multiple weaknesses, they should make a recommendation for each weakness they have noted. All recommendations made must be supported by a clear rationale to justify why they have been suggested – and be supported by a cost benefit analysis.

Whilst it may not be possible to identify all benefits in terms of cost, as some may be qualitative, it is essential that all costs are at least identified, and quantified in monetary terms, even if estimates are used. For example, if the recommendation includes staff training for three days, the cost of the employee time must be taken into account as well as the cost of training, as this is a lost opportunity cost. It is much better to make an approximation of difficult to measure costs than to just ignore them altogether.

It is perfectly acceptable for the student to make assumptions as to salaries, saving etc. For example the learner may assume an employee is earning £20 per hour and they are required to train for 30 hours – the cost then being 30 x £20 (plus 15% on-costs – employers' national insurance contribution and staff benefits).

The impact of the recommendations upon the staff in the accounting function should also be considered, and systems put into place to ensure that staff have the necessary skills and knowledge through appropriate training to ensure they can use the accounting systems effectively. This training could be provided by internal or external courses, and could also include the use of manuals or other written guidance and help menus in computer software.

Any recommendation made must always consider the need for staff training.

Not specifically assessed

- No management issues will be assessed – supervision, delegation or motivation.

- Management styles will not be assessed.

- Implementation and review of the recommendations will not be assessed.

HOW TO USE THIS WORKBOOK

This workbook contains tasks for you, the student, to complete. By completing these tasks, and then reviewing the suggested solutions, you are learning about organisations, their accounting systems and their internal controls. These are the areas that make up the standards of competence, learning outcomes and assessment criteria of this paper.

You should work through the book taking each chapter in turn; stopping and thinking about each of the tasks presented to you. If you are in a class at a training provider, your tutor may ask you to discuss a task and see how many answers a group of you can come up with before reviewing them with you. If you are studying on your own then you might like to jot down as many ideas as you can, perhaps using the Internet to help you, before looking at the suggested answers.

At the end of each chapter there is an explanation of how to complete the relevant section of your report based on what you have covered in the chapter. This should be supplemented by advice from your tutor and/or assessor and you should ensure that you let your assessor see your work as you progress so that they can provide you with appropriate advice and feedback.

chapter 1:
THE BASIC PRINCIPLES OF INTERNAL CONTROLS AND ACCOUNTING SYSTEMS

chapter coverage 📖

In this chapter we will look at the basic principles of this paper – Internal Controls and Accounting Systems (ISYS).

We will review the learning outcomes of the two units and how to ensure that they are covered within the management report you are required to write in order to demonstrate competence in the standards.

We will also discuss a critical question when considering how to write the required report – should you base this around the organisation in which you work or an AAT Case Study? If you wish to complete it based on your own organisation there are certain factors to consider which we will review.

We will also review the Assessment Process so that you are aware of the demands on both you the student and your assessor in order that competence be demonstrated and assessed.

We will also review the approach to the ISYS report for students for whom English is not their first language and where you may be able to access additional advice and support if this relates to you.

Finally we will review some Frequently Asked Questions (FAQs) from this unit to (hopefully!) address any concerns that you may have on how to complete it.

THE ISYS MANAGEMENT REPORT

The ISYS project should be presented to your assessor as a report to management, with appropriate appendices. It must be written in a professional business style, and analyse the learning outcomes identified for this paper. These are:

- Understand the role of accounting within the organisation.
- Understand the importance and use of internal control systems.
- Evaluate the accounting system and identify areas for improvement.
- Conduct an ethical evaluation of the accounting system.
- Conduct a sustainability evaluation of the accounting system.
- Make recommendations to improve the accounting system.

This report can either be based on the organisation where you work or on an AAT written Case Study that your assessor can provide you with.

The report should be approximately 4,000 to 5,000 words in length (excluding your appendices); however this is only a guide. You and your assessor should ensure that your work covers all of the standards required in this unit in order that it be assessed as competent.

If your work is significantly under this count then it probably does not contain all the areas required. Map it carefully to the assessment criteria (see Chapter 7) and ensure all are covered sufficiently. If your finished report is much longer than this then it may be too wordy or you may have more in it than required. Ask your assessor for advice and ensure that your word count does **not** include your appendices.

The report must also be written in an appropriate format and include certain sections. The final version, which **must be word processed**, might include:

- Title Page
- Contents
- Terms of Reference
- Executive Summary
- Methodology
- Introduction to the Organisation
- The Accounts Department
- Review of the Accounting System
- Ethical Evaluation of the Accounting System
- Sustainability Review of the Accounting System
- Internal Control and an Analysis of Fraud
- Recommendations to Improve
- Cost Benefit Analysis
- Appendices

This workbook will take you through the key areas of the report, explaining each in detail, and how to achieve competence in them. It will also guide you through the compilation of the report and the sections required to be in it and why.

It will then explain to you how to map your work to the standards and ensure all areas are covered. In each section it explains which standards must be covered and gives guidance and support on how to do this.

Once you are a fully qualified AAT Technician an employer would expect you to be able to produce a professional management report in an appropriate style and format. By the time you have completed this unit these are the skills and knowledge you will have gained.

OWN ORGANISATION OR CASE STUDY?

Own organisation

If you work in an organisation where you can investigate whether the accounting systems and controls in place are appropriate to the organisation, and report to management on them, then this is the best approach to take. This will not only mean you produce a good report that is competent but also that you have added value to your organisation and ensured your recommendations are noted by management.

You may be thinking that your organisation is too large or too controlled by management for any of your recommendations to be implemented – this does not matter. Implementation of any recommendations made is not a requirement of this unit.

The main outcome of your work should be that you have investigated the accounting systems and the internal controls in place within it and made recommendations for improvement. By having done this you will have gained a great deal of knowledge about your work place and this can only enhance your value to your organisation.

You may also be thinking that there are no improvements to be made, perhaps your workplace is already perfect! It is usual that after further research some improvements can be identified – again, we stress that they do not have to be implemented. If, however, you complete your research and find that there are no recommendations to make then this is acceptable (though very rare!). As long as in your detailed report you have covered all the learning outcomes in sufficient detail then your work should be assessed as competent.

Note that in order to complete this work based on your work place you will require your **manager's approval**. They will need to sign an **authenticity statement** once you have presented them with your final report to testify that it is based on the work place and is a true representation of it. Your manager will also be required to testify that the work is your own. You must have their approval to do this, as without this statement your assessor can not assess your work.

If, after consideration, you find that you are unable to investigate all the learning outcomes in your own organisation then you may find that a Case Study is for you.

It may be the case that your employer does not know you are studying or that you are not working in an accounting role and therefore you are not able to investigate and report on an accounting system. If this is the case then an AAT Case Study scenario may be more appropriate for you.

Case Study

In completing your work based on a Case Study you will need to ensure that it reads as if you work in the organisation described in the case study. Your final report should be no different to that of a student who is writing based on their own organisation.

The AAT will present the Case Study to you in an electronic format via the AAT LearnPlus. It will consist of several documents describing a fictitious organisation, its accounts department and its staff.

You must read through the entire Case Study and assume all the information contained within it is your own knowledge of the work place.

You should complete each section of your report on the assumption that your assessor has no prior knowledge of the organisation.

Your assessor will take the place of the work place manager and must produce an authenticity statement at the end once competence has been achieved. In order that they can do this, you will need to provide them with drafts of your work so that they can give advice, support and feedback but also be assured it is your own unaided work. You must be in constant contact with them throughout the process.

Case Study Advice

This Workbook features specific advice within each chapter on how to use the Case Study to complete your work. Look out for the paragraphs formatted like this.

If you do select to complete your report based on an AAT Case Study then be aware that once you have access to the scenario on the AAT's LearnPlus system you will then have to submit a report for formal assessment within four months of the scheduled assessment start date. During those four months you are permitted to have up to five 'formative guidance meetings' with your tutor where you can receive guidance on your progress to date.

Having reviewed your first submission, if your assessor assesses you as 'not yet competent', then you may have four further opportunities to submit more

---

supporting evidence (at the discretion of the assessor). Submissions of additional evidence should be completed within six months of the scheduled assessment start date or at the discretion of the assessor.

Note: The time limits, the number of times reports/evidence may be submitted and the assessment guidance included in this chapter are based on the AAT guidance in force at the time this book was published (June 2013). You should check these details with your assessor and read the latest AAT guidance to ensure that you are aware of any changes to the assessment guidance following publication of this workbook.

ASSESSMENT STANDARDS

The ISYS project is assessed once completed by the student. As part of the assessment process the assessor is required to confirm that the work meets the following criteria (VACS):

- **V**alid – it meets the standards

- **A**uthentic – it is the student's own, unaided work

- **C**urrent – it has been written recently and reflects how the organisation currently operates

- **S**ufficient – it investigates the key areas in sufficient detail to meet the standards

Its **validity** is assured by the student mapping the work to the learning outcomes. This means that you must cross-reference all your work to the criteria of this unit. To do this you must number all the pages and paragraphs of your work and write the relevant paragraph number into a mapping document next to the criteria they refer to.

Authenticity is assured by the student and the assessor working together through the project. This process starts with the student submitting a proposal to the assessor, which the assessor feeds back on. Your assessor should then review drafts of your work as you progress and provide further feedback on this. This aids them in being sure your work is your own and unaided. It is worth also noting that they may not be able to authenticate work that is presented to them as a fully completed report where they have not seen and fed back on drafts as they were written.

For students completing this report based on their work place they then require a signed and dated statement, on company headed paper, from their manager testifying that the work is their own, unaided and a true reflection of the work place. If this can not be obtained then the Case Study would be a better option for the student.

For Case Study students the assessor will act as their manager. In this situation the assessor will sign and date a witness statement to the same effect as the work place manager above. It is even more critical that for Case Study reports the student submits drafts and the assessor feeds back on them.

Authenticity may also be confirmed through a final interview between the student and the assessor once the work has been submitted and assessed. In the final interview the assessor asks the student questions about the work they have completed. This enables them to confirm the work is their own and unaided. The final interview may also be used by the assessor to strengthen any weaker areas of the learning outcomes and assessment criteria.

Currency concerns whether the report is up-to-date and relevant in the work place. It is worth remembering this and ensuring your work is based on current issues in your organisation.

Sufficiency relates to the work covering the learning outcomes in sufficient detail for the assessor to be sure that it meets the standards required. For some of the assessment criteria it may be necessary to include technical notes in the appendices of your report, to explain a point fully, as you have not been able to do this in the body of your report. This is acceptable and your assessor should be able to advise you on this.

THE ASSESSMENT PROCESS

The assessment process has already been discussed in this chapter but it is important that you, the student, understand it fully so that you can ensure you complete your work appropriately, get it assessed promptly and complete this unit and your Level 4 Diploma.

The first stage of the process is that the assessor should discuss the project with you and review your initial ideas. This is a **project proposal** and can either be done through you submitting a formal written document or in a one to one discussion with your assessor. Either way a documented record of this must be kept as it might be reviewed by the AAT once competence has been achieved.

The assessor may, at this stage, agree with you an **assessment plan**. This should cover how the report will be completed and a timescale. It should include a plan as to when each draft will be submitted for feedback and when the final version will be ready.

The assessment plan is just that – a plan. It will be revised and updated as the project progresses and again is a key part of the document audit trail required by the AAT for this unit.

Once the approach to the report has been agreed then **drafts** should be submitted to your assessor for review and formative guidance in the form of

BPP
LEARNING MEDIA

feedback. This ensures that you keep on the right track as you complete the work and that the assessor can be sure your work is your own and unaided.

You may be assessed as competent on a first submission however most students will require more than one assessment. After each assessment your assessor will feed back to you via Learn Plus (at their discretion). You can then make adjustments to your report and load this back onto Learn Plus for the next assessment. You can have up to a maximum of five assessments

Do not complete too much of the report before submitting it. Any assessor might be suspicious of a fully completed report being handed in for assessment if they have not worked with and guided the student through its completion.

Your assessor can only provide you with a maximum of five formative guidance sessions and/or written feedback so you should ensure that you address their comments within your report after each session.

Your assessor should explain to you at the start of this paper's completion exactly how and in what format this formative guidance will take place.

One of the requirements the AAT place on assessors is that they ensure you have **mapped your work to the required criteria**. This is covered in detail in Chapter 7; for now it is important to understand that your work will not be accepted without this mapping. It must be mapped to all the learning outcomes in order that it can be assessed.

Once a **full version** of your report is ready then it must be **professionally presented** and submitted for assessment via AAT LearnPlus. It must be submitted with your **manager's authenticity statement** (if completing the report on your workplace) and with your full mapping to the standards. It must include all the formatting requirements discussed later in this Workbook and all the required sections, **each starting on a new page**.

The assessor then undertakes a formal assessment of the work. They do this in a number of different ways and are, in essence, confirming the VACS criteria discussed earlier in this chapter. This is then documented and fed back to you via LearnPlus.

The final stage of the assessment process for this unit then takes place once the assessor has assessed the work to the VACS criteria. This might take the format of a **final interview** which takes place between the student and the assessor to discuss the work, its completion and key outcomes.

The assessor can also use the final interview to ask questions regarding any areas of the learning outcomes that were weak in the final report. This gives them a small amount of flexibility in their assessment although it would not be expected that this be used to assess to sufficient detail the key areas of the report. It is used more to test and probe further a point and this aids them in confirming the authenticity of the work.

Then the assessor submits the work for **Internal Moderation (IM)**. This is an internal quality assurance system required by all such qualifications.

The centre IM checks a sample of all assessors' work in order to confirm that it is to standard and to provide appropriate feedback and support. Although it would not be expected that the assessor's decision of competence be overturned as a result of this, it could happen and you could be asked to amend your work or update it.

Again, it is rare that the overall assessment decision be overturned but this does, on occasion, occur. If this is the case your assessor will contact you with information about the additional work required for competence.

Once this period has passed, or your work is scrutinised and accepted, your provisional result will then be updated.

As highlighted earlier in this chapter, one thing to note is that at the assessor's discretion, you may have further opportunities to submit additional supporting evidence if you are initially assessed as not competent (following your first submission of a substantial report for formal assessment).

The assessment process

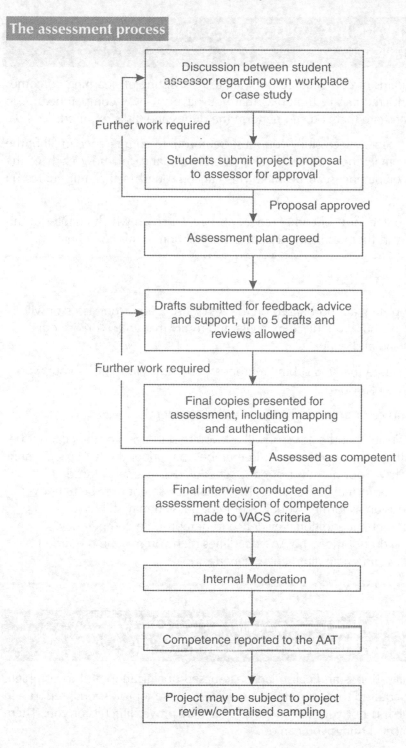

Discussion between student assessor regarding own workplace or case study

Further work required

Students submit project proposal to assessor for approval

Proposal approved

Assessment plan agreed

Drafts submitted for feedback, advice and support, up to 5 drafts and reviews allowed

Further work required

Final copies presented for assessment, including mapping and authentication

Assessed as competent

Final interview conducted and assessment decision of competence made to VACS criteria

Internal Moderation

Competence reported to the AAT

Project may be subject to project review/centralised sampling

THE AAT LEARNING OUTCOMES AND STANDARDS OF COMPETENCE

The AAT standards of competence (or syllabus), consisting of learning outcomes and assessment criteria, are the areas that you have to show competence in, in order to demonstrate that you can perform the duties and tasks required.

To complete a paper successfully you must demonstrate competence in all of the standards of competence. The AAT also publish guidance on how each of the standards of competence can be met. This can be found in the unit guides on their website.

A full set of the standards of competence, plus guidance on which chapter of this companion covers them, is included in the introduction to this companion.

Case Study Advice

If you are completing a report based on the AAT Case Study, your assessor will take the place of your work place manager and testify that your work is your own, unaided and authentic.

It is critical therefore that you submit a proposal and drafts to them as your work progresses and get feedback.

This aids your assessor in confirming your work is authentic.

There is a possibility that the assessor will ask you to start again as they cannot be sure of the authenticity of your work. Remember that under the ICAS assessment rules you only have four months from the scheduled assessment start date to submit a report for formal assessment. The initial assessment may be a 'not yet competent' decision as further work is required, but you may still have opportunities to submit additional evidence to demonstrate competency. However, if you do not meet the AAT deadlines then you may be required to start your work again on an alternative scenario.

THE ICAS PROJECT FOR STUDENTS FOR WHOM ENGLISH IS NOT THEIR FIRST LANGUAGE

The AAT qualification is an English language-based qualification and to complete it you will be required to demonstrate an ability to write a professional report – in English. If English is not your first language this may prove difficult for you. There are several practical things you can do:

(a)   Talk to your assessor – they will be able to advise and support you (but note they can not proof read or correct your work for you).

(b) Ask a friend or colleague to be a mentor – they are able to proof read your work and advise you on any amendments that can be made.

(c) Turn on your spellchecker – the finished report needs to be typed so complete it using a word processing package with the spellchecker and grammar checker turned on to highlight any errors made.

(d) Contact your AAT members' society – they may be able to provide you with an AAT member volunteer who can proof read your work and advise you on the completion of it.

Your assessor must be confident that your finished and final report is professional and in good business English. They can not report it as competent unless it is. If you need help and support to do this then raise this as early as possible in the process.

FAQS

1 **What areas must my project cover?** – The analysis of an accounting system, a review of internal controls and the opportunity for fraudulent activities, recommendations to improve the system and a cost benefit analysis of the recommendations. An example of the sections you could include were covered earlier in this chapter.

2 **Does this have to be based on my work place?** – No, the AAT produces Case Studies on which you may base your report but in this case it should look no different to a report based on a real organisation. To complete it you will have to assume you work in the organisation and all the information contained in the scenario is knowledge you have obtained from working there. An AAT written sample Case Study, and a sample of a student's first draft completed report, are included in the back of this workbook.

3 **How long should the finished report be?** – Approximately 4,000 to 5,000 words; however you must cover all the learning outcomes and lay the report out in a certain format so if you are significantly under or over this amount talk to your assessor for advice.

4 **Should I write the whole report then submit it for assessment?** – No. This is dangerous as your assessor must be sure your work is authentic and if you do this they will be unable to be sure. Also it is very difficult to produce a perfect report first time.

Submit a proposal and drafts to your assessor and get feedback and support as you complete your work. This will not only make the process easier for you but ensure they are comfortable that your work is your own.

5 **My English is not very good – will this affect my competence?** – It could do, yes. Your final report must be in English and be in a professional written style. See the section in this chapter on students for whom English is not

their first language for advice and support on how to ensure your work is to an acceptable standard.

6   **Must my project cover all the learning outcomes?** – Yes. In order to be judged competent you must cover all the criteria sufficiently. See the chapters on the assessment process and mapping to assist you in doing this.

7   **My manager won't or can't produce an authentication statement, what can I do?** – If you have completed your project on your work place and your manager will not produce an appropriate authenticity statement, signed and dated on company headed paper, you do not have permission to submit your project based on your place of work. Without this statement your assessor will not be able to assess your work and so you would be asked to start your project again, perhaps based on a Case Study. It is important therefore that you gain your manager's consent before commencing your project using your own work place. If you are unable to obtain a manager's authentication statement you must let your assessor know as soon as possible.

8   **I am completing my project using the Case Study, who is my work place manager and how can they authenticate my work?** – When you complete the project based on the scenario in a Case Study your assessor takes on the role of work place manager and as part of the assessment process they will produce an authenticity statement. It is vital therefore that you submit a proposal and drafts of your work as you complete it so that they are able to testify that the work is your own and unaided.

9   **What is an assessment plan and must I complete one?** – An assessment plan is the result of a negotiation between you and your assessor to plan when and how you are going to complete each phase of the project and submit a final version of your work. It is an invaluable tool to carefully plan how you can complete the overall report. You do not need to keep exactly to the plan, it can be reviewed and updated as you progress.

10 **What is a project proposal and must I complete one?** – A project proposal is where you set out to your assessor your initial thoughts and ideas regarding your project. It is vital as it ensures that your assessor can judge whether your project will be appropriate and that you are not proposing too large or small an area of the accounting system to investigate. It allows your assessor to provide you with valuable feedback and support and is a key part of the authentication process.

11 **What is the final interview and what format will it take?** – The final interview is the last part of the assessment process and is where the assessor asks you questions about the work you have produced. It can aid them in authenticating your work and strengthen any minor areas of weakness so that they can be sure of the sufficiency of your competence. It should take the format of an interview, where your assessor will ask you questions and

you provide answers. It will be recorded – either written down or voice recorded – and if written you will be asked to confirm that the written evidence is a true reflection of the interview by signing and dating it. A final interview is not required for every student and your assessor will decide whether it is required in your case.

12 **How do I map my work and why must I do so?** – Mapping your work is where you inform the assessor of the paragraph number that covers each of the learning outcomes. This is important first, so that you can be sure that all the criteria are covered (if you can't map to one of them then you have missed it out and need to add a paragraph to include it!) and also to ensure that you have a good understanding of what you have gained competence in, by producing this work. To map your work take a copy of the learning outcomes and assessment criteria (see earlier) and reference each paragraph number to them.

13 **Can my project be a series of paragraphs, each addressing the learning outcomes in turn?** – No. This is not an appropriate way to produce a professional management report and would not be judged as competent as you will have not demonstrated an ability to write one. Instead, your report should be structured around the sections as outlined in this workbook.

14 **What is Internal Verification/Moderation?** – This is an internal quality assurance check. Each AAT Approved Assessment Centre has an internal verifier or moderator who is responsible for ensuring that work reported to the AAT as competent has been appropriately assessed and is actually competent. They do this through a variety of processes and you may have your assessed work reviewed or your final interview observed. If they do not agree with an assessment decision this will be communicated to you either by the AAT directly or your assessor and the additional work required to achieve competence will be discussed.

15 **I can not see how to include all the assessment criteria and learning outcomes in my report – what do I do?** – First of all you should discuss this with your assessor. They will review the mapping you have completed and also they understand the technical requirements of the standards. They will advise you but you should remember that if you are unable to cover all the assessment criteria fully and sufficiently in the body of your report you can include technical notes in the appendices to supplement and strengthen them. This should only be by exception however and not the rule and your assessor is best placed to advise you on this.

16 **What is formative guidance and why is it limited?** – Under the AAT rules of assessment of this unit there is a maximum of five formative guidance feedbacks that can be provided to you by your assessor. This may be in the form of meetings or written feedback with or from your assessor. In each case your assessor should review the work you have completed to date and

provide you with guidance on how it should be amended and what to complete next. This is limited to a maximum of five sessions to ensure that the work completed is your own and not as a result of too much assessor input. If, after five guidance sessions, your work is still not ready for assessment then your assessor may advise you that you are not yet ready to complete this unit and that you should undertake further development before attempting it again.

17 **What is assessment and why is it limited?** – Under the AAT rules of assessment in this unit, in addition to the five maximum formative guidance sessions, your assessor can then undertake a maximum number of assessments as specified by the AAT. **You should check the guidance provided by the AAT to see what the current maximum is.** At the time of writing this book, the assessor may permit a student up to four further opportunities to submit additional evidence following the initial submission. If, after these additional submissions, your work is still not yet competent it may be that your assessor advises you that you are not yet ready to complete this unit and that you need to undertake further development before attempting it again.

18 **How long do I have to complete my report?** – If you are completing the report on an AAT Case Study then you have up to four months from the assessment start date to submit your report. Once this period has elapsed you may find access to the scenario blocked such that you will need to start this unit again on an alternative one. If you are completing this report in your workplace, your assessor will advise you of the time constraints in place; they are likely to be similar. If you do not complete your report within these time limits then you may be required to start this unit again.

chapter 2:
INTRODUCTION TO THE ORGANISATION

---

chapter coverage 📖

In this chapter we will be looking at various types of organisation and the differences between them. We will then look at organisation structure as there are many different structure types and these will influence the organisation's culture and how it operates.

Organisations are also influenced by the stakeholders in the organisation – these are groups who are in some way affected by the organisation's actions. Stakeholder groups include employees, customers, suppliers and the community within which the organisation exists. Stakeholders can be categorised as either internal or external groups and we will look at how the organisation must react to the changing needs and demands of these groups.

Finally we will look at the regulatory framework within which the organisation exists and the impact that this will have on it.

The last section of this chapter will then explain how to include all of the above in your report, and to ensure that you explain them in relation to the organisation you have chosen to analyse, whether your own or an AAT Case Study.

ORGANISATION TYPES

There are many different types of organisation, most of which you can choose to base your ISYS report on. You should be able to identify these different types and recognise which your chosen organisation is and why that affects how it is structured and how it operates.

Most organisation types can be grouped into two distinct sectors:

- The public sector
- The private sector

And each of these sectors consists of a range of organisations who have different, distinct characteristics.

The public sector

Organisations operating within the public sector include central government, local government and businesses owned by the government. An example of a business owned by the government would be NHS Direct. The number of businesses owned by the government (often known as Nationalised Businesses) has shrunk considerably over the last 25 years, however, the recent banking crisis did see the government taking all or part ownership of a number of UK Banks.

Public sector organisations typically have very different objectives to those in the private sector as they are often responsible for providing a service rather than selling a product. For example, local government is responsible for many services including:

- Waste collection and disposal
- Street lighting
- Library services
- Museums
- Paths and parks
- Licensing

The private sector

Organisations in the private sector include the following:

- Sole traders
- Partnerships
- Private limited companies (Ltd)
- Public limited companies (Plc)

They primarily exist to make profits for the owners, through the provision of goods and services to paying customers.

Sole traders and partnerships differ from limited companies because their liability is unlimited. Unlimited liability means that the owners are personally liable for all of the debts of the business.

A **sole trader** is an organisation that is owned and run by one individual (the proprietor) and where there is no legal distinction between the owner and the business. The proprietor takes all profits and suffers all losses (subject to taxation). All the assets of the business are owned by the proprietor and all debts of the business are their debts and they must pay them from their personal resources. The proprietor has unlimited liability so that, if the business fails, they are personally liable for all its debts. It is a 'sole' proprietorship in the sense that the proprietor has no partners.

A **partnership** is a method of trading which arises where a number of sole traders trade together. A partnership is defined in the Partnership Act 1890 as 'the relation which subsists between persons carrying on a business in common with a view of profit'. Most partnerships consist of between two and twenty partners although the large accountancy and legal partnerships have many more partners than this. Most partnerships also have unlimited liability.

A **private limited company** is a legal person that exists in its own right. This means that the company's finances are separate from the owners' personal finances. A company will therefore have shareholders – who may be individuals or other companies – who are generally not responsible for the debts of the business but may lose the money invested in the business if it were to fail. A private limited company must use the letters Ltd after its name and is not able to offer shares for sale to the general public.

A **public limited company** is an organisation that can offer shares for sale to the general public and its shares can be traded on the Stock Exchange. Such an organisation will use the letters Plc after its name. A public limited company must have at least two shareholders and must issue shares to the public of at least £50,000 before it can legally trade.

Different types of organisations have different rules regarding the preparation and publication of accounts.

A **franchise** is an organisation type where the success of one business is exploited by selling the company name and product to individuals wishing to invest in it by trading under the organisation's name. It is a method of obtaining rapid, often international, growth. Successful franchises include Subway and McDonalds. The franchisee will invest in the business, buying from the franchisor an almost pre-packaged business including the company name, suppliers, logo etc and will then operate the franchise paying a regular fee to the franchiser to cover the royalty of using the trademark name and an amount in respect of training and advisory services.

Task 1

What are the common aims and objectives of most types of organisation? Write down as many as you can before reviewing the suggested answers at the back of this workbook.

What are the differences in the aims and objectives between public and private sector organisations? Again, take some time to think about this and write down as many differences as you can before reviewing the answers.

How does the organisation type affect the behaviour of the organisation? Think about two very distinct organisation types to help you with this – perhaps a small local charitable trust and a large multinational plc.

The third sector

A third business sector exists which is made up of a group of organisations that are not strictly within either the public or the private sector. Organisations in this sector share common characteristics in that they:

- Are non-governmental
- Are value-driven
- Principally reinvest any financial surpluses to advance social, environmental or cultural objectives.

Examples include:

- Cooperatives
- Trusts
- Charities

Cooperatives are defined as 'An autonomous association of persons united voluntarily to meet their common economic, social and cultural needs and aspirations through a jointly owned and democratically controlled enterprise'. In short, a cooperative is an organisation owned and controlled equally by the people who use its services or who work in it. It is a legal entity which shares its earnings with its members as dividends and those members are often bound by common social or ethical principles. An example of a cooperative in the UK is The Cooperative Group.

www.co-operative.coop/aboutus/

Charities are organisations that take a distinct legal form and are run mainly by volunteers. To register as a charity with the Charity Commission, and thus obtain a special tax status, the charity must prove that it provides a benefit to the public. The law must recognise its aims, purposes and or objectives to be charitable and a number of rules and regulations must be obeyed to gain and then retain charitable status. Charities can also register as companies, in which case they must also comply with company law.

www.charity-commission.gov.uk

Organisations also differ from each other due to factors other than ownership and the organisation's aims and objectives.

Task 2

What other factors, apart from ownership and aims and objectives, affect an organisation?

Think about what makes one organisation different from another and list as many differences as you can. All these factors impact on how an organisation operates.

Review the suggested answers at the back of this workbook once you have done this.

ORGANISATION STRUCTURES

Many of the factors you will have listed as part of Task 2 will affect the structure of an organisation. There are many different possible structures, and these are often affected by the size and age of the organisation. The structure of an organisation will affect how it operates and performs; an inappropriate structure can hinder the success of the organisation.

The structure of an organisation can be described as either flat or tall. A **flat** structure will not have many levels of management so the organisation chart would be quite flat, with each manager having many staff working for them (this is known as a wide span of control), and few management levels from the bottom of the organisation to the top. Organisations with flat structures can also have distinct operating divisions, perhaps with each having their own accounting functions. This type of organisation could also be said to be a decentralised organisation.

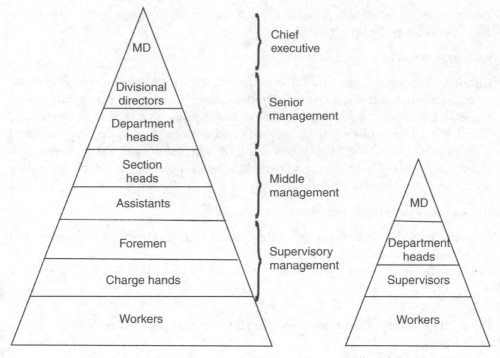

Tall and flat organisations

A **tall** organisation structure would be the opposite, with many levels of management and each manager would only be responsible for a small number of staff (a narrow span of control) A tall organisation can also be referred to as hierarchical – with many levels of hierarchy of management. A good example of an organisation with such a structure would be a government department, with many levels of managers and thousands of employees.

Often tall organisations are structured into pillars of expertise, so have centralised accounting functions (see Chapter 3).

The trend in modern organisation structures is to flatten or delayer, removing tiers of management. No one structure is right or wrong, it must fit the organisation type and there are advantages and disadvantages of each. In your report analysing your chosen organisation you must be sure to ensure that you review whether the current organisation structure is appropriate for the type of organisation you are analysing, and whether any improvements can be recommended.

Task 3

What are the advantages of a tall organisation structure?
What are the advantages of a flat organisation structure?

Write down as many advantages as you can think of, reviewing again our explanations of these organisation types set out above. Review the suggested answers at the back of this workbook once you have done this.

Centralised organisations are those where the decision making power and authority are held at one central location, usually a Head Office function. Support functions such as the accounts department are also centralised, and will complete tasks for the whole organisation.

A **decentralised** organisation is one where the decision making power lies in each part of the business, perhaps within each division, factory, shop etc. In this type of organisation it is much harder to control the decisions made by staff, but easier to adapt to local markets and make innovative decisions regarding the organisation.

ORGANISATION STAKEHOLDERS

A stakeholder is anyone who is affected by the actions of the organisation. Stakeholders can be either internal or external to the organisation and directly or indirectly affected by its actions. There are many stakeholders common to most organisation types such as employees, customers, suppliers and owners but different organisations will also have stakeholders unique to them.

Task 4

List as many internal stakeholders to an organisation as you can.

List as many external stakeholders to an organisation as you can.

For each of the above consider what information needs the stakeholders may have, and how an organisation might meet these needs.

Try and break stakeholder groups down into subgroups with the same or similar information needs. For example do not just put employees as a stakeholder group. Different groups of employees may have differing information needs. Once complete review our suggested answers at the back of this workbook.

Stakeholders have important information needs and organisations must ensure that they communicate appropriately with them, though this may be through many different methods. The accounting systems of an organisation will have an important role in this and as part of your analysis and investigation into the accounting system you will be expected to consider how it meets the stakeholders' needs and what information it can provide.

Stakeholders also affect the ethics and culture of organisations. A good example of an organisation which has a large stakeholder group that may wield influence over its ethics and culture would be a football club such as Manchester United or Liverpool Football Club. A large stakeholder group, who as a whole take a deep interest in the actions of the organisation, would be the fans. An interesting argument would be how much power and influence they can wield over the organisation – think about how often fans influence decisions regarding the managers of the club or even, in the case of the two examples above, the owners.

Another example would be the John Lewis partnership which is owned and run by its employees. All permanent employees become partners of the organisation and share in its profits. This ownership has a clear impact on the aims, objectives and ethics and culture of the organisation.

These examples also highlight the need for good communication with large and/or powerful stakeholder groups.

THE REGULATORY FRAMEWORK OF ACCOUNTING

There are many regulations affecting how organisations operate, both within the accounting and wider business environment.

The way in which companies prepare their annual financial statements is regulated both by the law and the accounting profession. The purpose of this regulation is to try to ensure that the financial statements of different companies and different types of businesses are as comparable as possible.

Companies Act

The Companies Act 2006 sets out the financial reporting framework under which financial statements should be prepared in the UK. It also contains specific requirements regarding how accounting records should be kept, and how the annual accounts should be distributed and filed. In recent years, there has been a focus on strengthening disclosures: rules regarding the disclosure of directors' remuneration have been brought in, for example.

For this unit you are expected to demonstrate a basic knowledge only of accounting regulations and how they impact on an organisation and therefore you will not be required to demonstrate a detailed knowledge of the Companies Act.

BPP
LEARNING MEDIA

Accounting standards

As well as the legal regulation of companies' financial statements the accounting profession also regulates the preparation of financial statements by issuing accounting standards. The first UK accounting standards were produced around 40 years ago and were known as Statements of Standard Accounting Practice (SSAPs). The aim of the accounting standards is to reduce the variety of methods of dealing with accounting issues and to set out the best method to use in order to increase the comparability of the financial statements of different organisations.

A number of SSAPs are still in issue although the UK accounting framework is now under the control of the Accounting Standards Board which issues Financial Reporting Standards (FRSs) with the same aims as the old SSAPs. Companies must follow the requirements of SSAPs and FRSs when preparing financial statements but other non-corporate organisations have more flexibility. However, the SSAPs and FRSs do represent UK best accounting practice and are followed by sole traders and partnerships as well as companies not following International Standards (see below). UK accounting standards and UK company law (primarily the Companies Act we looked at earlier) are collectively known as UK Generally Accepted Accounting Practice (UK GAAP).

Accounting practice in the UK and elsewhere is increasingly influenced by **International Financial Reporting Standards (IFRSs)** and International Accounting Standards (IASs), issued by the International Accounting Standards Board (IASB).

Many companies are now preparing their financial statements under IFRSs which contain different terminology to that used in UK accounting standards. On 1 January 2012 the AAT moved from UK GAAP to IFRS terminology for its assessments.

For the purposes of this unit you are required to demonstrate knowledge of how the accounting standards will **impact on the organisation** and the way in which it prepares its financial accounts (see Chapter 3) and the influence they may have on controls (see Chapter 5). We include both terminology used in IFRSs and UK GAAP. Usually, where the term differs for each, IFRSs terminology will be shown first (since this is the AAT's preferred terminology) with the UK GAAP terminology shown in brackets for information.

You will not be tested on the detail of particular accounting standards.

Other legislation

There are many other legislative regulations that impact on the organisation, either as a result of UK Acts of Parliament or European Directives. These may include:

- Taxation regulations including VAT, Corporation tax and PAYE for employees.

- Data protection law as set out in the Data Protection Act 1998.

- Late payment law as set out in the Late Payment of Commercial Debt (Interest) Act 1998.

- Health and Safety – The Health and Safety Executive are responsible in the UK for enforcing a variety of laws regarding safe and healthy work practices and places. www.hse.gov.uk

- Industry regulations – every industry has regulations that affect how it operates and, possibly, how it disposes of its waste. As part of your report you should include information regarding the regulations that affect your chosen organisation.

Accounting policies

Organisations also adopt their own accounting policies – rules as to how they construct their management and financial accounts. These are discussed in more detail in Chapter 3.

REPORT: INTRODUCTION TO THE ORGANISATION

To cover the outcomes of this chapter in your report you will need to write between one and two pages providing a brief outline of the organisation you have chosen to investigate and details of its current type and structure. You may find it appropriate to include an organisation chart in an appendix to help you explain the structure. Ensure you explain the ownership of the organisation and the key stakeholders affected by its actions.

Ensure that you clearly describe the aims and objectives of the organisation – to assist with this you may be able to research mission statements from its website or from published records and accounts.

You must also include a summary of the regulatory framework in which it operates, providing examples of both accounting and non-accounting regulations (if appropriate) with which it must comply.

Your report must be written in the third person only (that is no 'I' or 'we' or 'he' or 'she').

The report should be a series of short paragraphs showing each area of investigation. When you have completed it you should be able to map your work to the assessment criteria – see Chapter 7 on mapping your work to help you with this.

You must ensure that you include copies of any documents referred to in your report (for example an organisation chart showing the structure in place) in your appendices. This is important reference material for the person reading the final report.

Finally, if you feel that any of the relevant assessment criteria have not been covered specifically by this section, you should include technical notes in an appendix. Your assessor will be able to advise you whether this is required.

Checklist

- Write up your research of each area of investigation as outlined above.

- Ensure you cover:

    - A brief background to the organisation
    - Its aims and objectives
    - External regulations affecting the organisation
    - External stakeholders

- Include copies of all relevant documents in the appendices.

- Write only in the third person.

- Use short, individually numbered paragraphs.

- Map your work to the assessment criteria.

Case Study Advice

When you have read the Case Study through you will notice most of the areas of the required research outlined above are clearly mentioned and some are implied. For example it may be helpful to construct an organisation chart from the information provided (to place in your appendices) to get a clear picture of the current organisation style and/or type.

You may also need to use your knowledge of common stakeholder groups in order to explain key stakeholders of the organisation and complete some research to understand the regulatory framework that might affect how it operates. Immerse yourself in the scenario and remember that the report must read in the same way as if it were your actual workplace. Use your skills, knowledge and imagination to supplement the case scenario if required.

The sample report at the back of this workbook will aid your understanding as to how to complete this. Remember to send your draft to your assessor for review – it will aid their authentication of your work and provide you with valuable feedback on your progress.

FAQS

1   **How much should I write in this section?** – This section should be between one and two pages in length and explain the organisation's ownership, structure, stakeholders (both internal and external) and the regulatory framework within which it operates. There is therefore a lot of competence to demonstrate so keep your work reasonably brief and do not write a history of the organisation, unless this helps explain it in the context of where it is today.

2   **What is an internal stakeholder?** – This is anyone who is affected by the actions of the organisation and is directly and internally linked to it. The term generally refers to employees, managers and supervisors for example. In the report you may split employees into different employee groups to enable you to better explain their relationship to the organisation.

3   **What is an external stakeholder?** – This is anyone who is affected by the actions of the organisation and is not internal to it. It can refer to many groups including customers, suppliers, the community, the government etc.

4   **How do I include external regulations?** – All organisations are bound by external regulations that affect how they operate. These include accounting and non-accounting regulations. Look at the industry that the organisation operates within and any regulations that may be specific to it. Talk to management within the organisation and also do some research on the internet. Include explanations of the regulations that affect the organisation.

5   **What appendices can I include for this section?** – The appendices to your report should be any documents that help explain the situation to the reader. Any diagrams should be included in the appendices and not in the body of the report. A good approach in this section would be to construct a simple organisation chart and include this to help explain how the organisation is structured.

6   **The AAT Case Study has limited information on this section, how do I supplement my writing?** – If you use what knowledge you have gained by working through this chapter you will see that general knowledge can supplement the Case Study. It may be that you can construct an organisation chart, from the information provided, and then conclude as to the structure of the organisation and whether the accounts department is centralised or decentralised. You can also use your knowledge, supplemented by careful reading of the scenario, to list the key stakeholders to the organisation, both internal and external, and to define their relationship to it.

chapter 3:
THE ACCOUNTS DEPARTMENT

―― **chapter coverage** 📖 ――

In this chapter we will look at the accounts department as a function of an organisation and review different approaches to such functions in the context of structure.

The trend in organisations has been, over recent years, to centralise functions such as accounts and even to outsource all or some of the role of the accounts team to third parties. We will consider the impact that this has on the organisation and how it operates.

We will also review the role of the accounts department and the differences between management and financial accounts. Both have a different focus, approach and meet different stakeholder needs.

We will also briefly look at the management of the accounts department and how this impacts on its culture.

Following on from the theme of stakeholders, discussed in the previous chapter, we will look at key stakeholders to the accounts department and how the department might communicate with both internal and external stakeholder groups.

In this section of report you will therefore be expected to review and explain the structure and approach to the accounts department within your chosen organisation and review whether it is appropriate to it. After this review you will be expected to make suitable recommendations as to how the organisation of the accounts department might be improved.

LEARNING OUTCOMES

1.1 – Describe the purpose, structure and organisation of the accounting function and its relationship with other functions within the organisation

1.2 – Explain the various business purposes for which the following accounting information is required:

- Statement of profit or loss
- Statement of cash flows
- Statement of financial position

1.4 – Explain how the accounting systems are affected by the organisational structure, systems, procedures and business transactions

3.1 – Identify an organisation's accounting system requirements including hardware and software packages

THE ACCOUNTS DEPARTMENT

The preparation of accounts is a key function in any organisation, whether within the public or the private sector and includes many activities which can, in larger organisations, also be functions in their own right. These include:

- Accounts receivable (sales ledger)
- Accounts payable (purchase ledger)
- Payroll
- Costing
- Budgeting

The main aim of any accounting function is to accurately and fully process all accounting transactions for the organisation, whilst avoiding processing any invalid transactions, so that the information provided to stakeholders is correct and up to date.

How an organisation's accounting function is organised and structured depends on many of the factors discussed in Chapter 2 including its size, age, ownership, stakeholders and objectives. These factors will also affect the specific tasks the function performs, for example the private sector will maintain detailed accounts for customers whereas the public sector will do so to a much lesser extent.

Organisations choose to keep functions such as accounting either centralised or decentralised and both approaches have their advantages and disadvantages.

Centralised functions

Centralisation is where an organisation chooses to place all staff who perform a particular function at the same location, regardless of where other activities are carried out. An example might be a large manufacturing organisation which chooses to have the accounts function sited at Head Office rather than in several different locations at the manufacturing sites.

Many organisations, such as Ford Motor Company, now choose to centralise such functions globally.

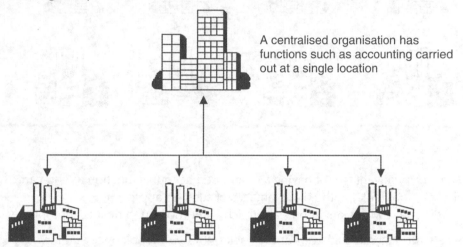

A centralised organisation has functions such as accounting carried out at a single location

Centralisation brings with it many advantages such as economies of scale as fewer staff overall are needed to complete the same amount of work. It may also bring disadvantages such as the creation of an 'Ivory Tower' function that is remote from the operational centres and has little or no involvement with the rest of the organisation.

Decentralisation

A decentralised approach to the accounting function would be where an organisation has chosen to have several separate accounts departments, perhaps one for each division or separate organisation entity such as factories. A decentralised approach often follows a structure and strategy where the organisation treats each of its parts as a separate profit making entity in its own right. Decentralisation may require more staff but can lead to better information flows and communication as the staff are based 'at site'. An example would be a manufacturing organisation with several factories, each with its own accounts team.

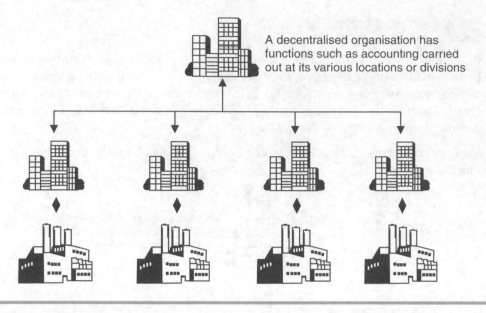

A decentralised organisation has functions such as accounting carried out at its various locations or divisions

Task 1

List as many advantages of having a centralised accounts function as you can.
What do you think are the disadvantages of such an approach?
What is your own organisation's approach – and do you think it is appropriate?

Review the suggested answers at the back of this workbook once you have completed this task.

Outsourcing

Many organisations take some, or more rarely all, of the functions carried out by an accounts department and not only centralise them but then choose to outsource this work to a third party, often under strict service level agreements (SLAs).

An example of a function that has seen an increase in outsourcing over recent years is payroll. Outsourcing is most popular for routine tasks, which are highly automated and rely on information technology for processing. As payroll skills and knowledge is also quite specialised it may be cheaper for small or medium sized organisations to 'buy in' the specialised knowledge from an organisation rather than employ staff with appropriate knowledge and experience. A payroll bureau will be able to share skilled staff across several organisations, producing economies of scale, and a cheaper service for customers.

BPP
LEARNING MEDIA

THE ROLE OF THE ACCOUNTS DEPARTMENT

The role of the accounts department is primarily to provide information. Either internally through financial and management accounting information, or externally through financial accounting information in the form of published accounts.

Financial accounting

Financial accounting is the process of producing financial statements for decision makers, that provide the reader with an overview of the financial performance of the organisation. The decision makers concerned with the financial statements of an organisation might include many of the key internal and external stakeholders discussed in Chapter 2. This might include the owners, government agencies, banks and suppliers.

Financial accountants prepare financial accounting information for publication to people both internal and external to the organisation. They summarise financial data taken from the organisation's accounting records and publish it in the form of reports. The preparation of such reports is governed by company law and accounting standards, as discussed in Chapter 2.

Financial accounting includes the preparation of:

Statement of profit or loss – The STATEMENT OF PROFIT OR LOSS of an organisation is a summary of the activity of the organisation during the year. It is, in simple terms:

INCOME minus EXPENSES equals PROFIT OR LOSS

If the income is greater than the expenses then a profit has been made. If the expenses exceed the income then a loss has been made.

However, despite the simple concept of the statement of profit or loss it is normally laid out in a particular manner.

Statement of profit or loss

	£	£
Revenue		44,000
Less Cost of sales		
Opening inventory	2,400	
Purchases	28,000	
	30,400	
Less closing inventory	(3,200)	
Cost of sales		(27,200)
Gross profit		16,800
Less Expenses		
Electricity	240	
Marketing	80	
Discount allowed	440	
Discount received	(280)	
Wages	10,400	
Travel	160	
Rent	600	
Telephone	320	
		(11,960)
Profit for the year		4,840

The GROSS PROFIT is the profit earned by the trading activities of the business. As you can see it is calculated as revenue less the cost of those sales.

The second part of the statement of profit or loss consists of a list of all of the EXPENSES of the business.

The PROFIT FOR THE YEAR is the final profit of the business after all of the expenses have been deducted.

Statement of financial position – Whereas the statement of profit or loss is a history of the transactions of the business during the accounting period the STATEMENT OF FINANCIAL POSITION is simply a 'snap shot' of the business on the final day of the accounting period.

The statement of financial position is a list of all of the assets, liabilities and capital of the business. It is also an expression of the accounting equation. Remember that the accounting equation is:

ASSETS minus LIABILITIES equals CAPITAL

The statement of financial position is a vertical form of the accounting equation. It lists and totals the assets of the business and deducts the liabilities. This total is then shown to be equal to the capital of the business.

Statement of financial position

	£	£	£
Non-current assets			10,200
Current assets:			
Inventory	3,200		
Receivables	3,800		
Bank	800		
		7,800	
Current liabilities:			
Payables		(2,400)	
Net current assets			5,400
			15,600
Long term liabilities:			
Loan			(2,000)
			13,600

Financed by:

	£
Opening capital	12,760
Add profit	4,840
	17,600
Less drawings	(4,000)
	13,600

The statement of financial position falls naturally into two parts which are the two sides of the ACCOUNTING EQUATION – 'assets minus liabilities' and 'capital'.

The NON-CURRENT ASSETS are always shown as the first assets on the being the major long-term assets of the business.

The CURRENT ASSETS of a business are its other shorter term assets. These are listed in particular order starting with the least liquid asset, inventory, followed by receivables and then finally the most liquid asset the bank account and then possibly followed by cash in hand or petty cash.

The CURRENT LIABILITIES of a business are the short term payables – the other title that is used for these in the UK is 'Creditors: amounts payable within one year'.

The NET CURRENT ASSETS figure is a sub-total of the current assets minus the current liabilities. The net current asset total is then added to the non-current asset total.

The LONG-TERM LIABILITIES are liabilities that are due to be paid after more than one year. In this case we have assumed that the loan is a long term loan, ie, repayable after more than one year. The total for long term liabilities is deducted from the total of non-current assets and net current assets to give the total shown on the statement of financial position. In terms of the accounting equation this is the total of the assets minus liabilities.

The CAPITAL section of the statement of financial position shows the amounts that are owed to the owner of the business. This consists of the amount of capital owed to the owner at the start of the accounting period plus the profit that the business has earned (this figure of £4,840 is the profit taken from the statement of profit or loss) less the drawings that the owner has taken out of the business during the accounting period. The total of the capital section will, of course, equal the total of the assets minus the liabilities.

Note that drawings are part of the statement of financial position and are not included as expenses – they are a reduction of the amount that is owed to the owner by the business.

Income and expenditure accounts

Sole traders, partnerships and companies all produce a statement of profit or loss and a statement of financial position. Other types of not-for-profit organisations such as clubs and societies do not prepare a statement of profit or loss showing a 'profit' as their aim is not necessarily to make a profit. However these organisations do produce something very similar known as an income and expenditure account which shows a 'surplus' if income exceeds expenditure. An example of an income and expenditure account together with its associated statement of financial position are shown below for illustration.

Income and expenditure account for Crowfield Rugby Club for the year ended 31 December 20X0

	£	£
Income:		
Subscription income		7,170
Bar profit		3,100
Dinner dance profit		400
		10,670
Less Expenditure		
Loss on sale of grass cutter	100	
Depreciation of grass cutter	250	
Rent and rates	1,300	
Electricity	2,040	
Groundsman's expenses	700	
Club secretary's expenses	900	
Fixtures fees	3,500	
Sundry expenses	200	
		(8,990)
Surplus of income over expenditure		1,680

Statement of financial position as at 31 December 20X0

	£	£
Non-current assets at cost		1,000
Less provision for depreciation		(250)
Net book value		750
Bar inventory	1,800	
Subscriptions in arrears	30	
Prepayment	300	
Bank	1,550	
		3,680
		4,430
Less Payables		
Subscriptions in advance	120	
Accruals	240	
		(360)
		4,070
		£
Accumulated fund at 1 January 20X0		2,390
Surplus of income over expenditure		1,680
Accumulated fund at 31 December 20X0		4,070

Manufacturing accounts

A further type of accounting statement that some manufacturing organisations will produce is a manufacturing account. This is a structured list of all of the expenses incurred in the production process culminating in the total cost of the goods manufactured in the period. An example of a manufacturing account is given below for illustration.

Manufacturing account for the year ended 31 March 20X1

	f	£
Opening inventory (stock) of raw materials		6,000
Purchases of raw materials		70,000
		76,000
Less closing inventory (stock) of raw materials		(8,000)
Direct materials used		68,000
Direct labour		36,000
Direct expenses		1,900
Prime cost		105,900
Production overheads:		
Supervisor's salary	17,000	
Factory rent	8,000	
Machinery depreciation	6,000	
Factory light and heat	4,000	
		35,000
		140,900
Add opening work in progress		4,000
		144,900
Less closing work in progress		(4,900)
Manufacturing cost of goods completed		140,000

Accounting policies

When final accounts are being prepared for an organisation they will be prepared according to company law, accounting standards and the organisation's own accounting policies. The organisation's accounting policies govern the precise way in which the rules set out in the accounting standards are applied to the organisation's particular circumstances.

For example, organisations are generally required to depreciate their non-current assets. However, the precise rate at which depreciation is applied is determined by the management of the organisation in the form of an accounting policy.

The choice of accounting policies that an organisation makes is fundamental to the picture shown by the final accounts and therefore an International Accounting Standard (IAS) has been issued on this area – IAS 8 *Accounting policies, changes in accounting estimates and errors*. (UK accounting standard FRS 18 *Accounting policies* also covers this area). You do not require detailed knowledge of IAS 8 (or FRS 18) for this unit.

Management accounting

Management accounting differs from financial accounting in that it is internally focused and is less bound by strict rules and reporting standards and more by the needs of the organisation's management.

Management accounting aims to provide management with financial information that they can use in order to make critical decisions that affect how the organisation is run. Management accountants prepare information solely for the use of internal stakeholders. This includes the preparation of information such as:

- Budgets
- Costing
- Standard costs
- Variance reports
- Ratio analysis
- Sales figures for products and or divisions
- Inventory levels
- Profitability reports
- Any other internal information prepared using financial data

All of the above management accounting reports would be used internally, within the organisation, by management to help them manage the organisation's profitability and cash flow. They will be used to make decisions on resourcing and may form part of performance management appraisal. For example, a stores manager might be set the objective to keep inventories to an acceptable level, especially in an organisation that holds perishable inventories such as food products.

Task 2

Research what internal management accounting reports are prepared within your own organisation.

What value to do they have? Think about how managers might use them to make decisions about the organisation.

What additional information might management need to make better, more informed decisions?

MANAGEMENT OF THE ACCOUNTS DEPARTMENT

How a department is managed has a large impact on the culture within it. In this context, culture can be regarded as 'The way we do things around here' and may be very different from the way an organisation might want it to be.

Management affect the culture within the organisation because they set the standard for how the organisation operates on a day to day basis. This is often what makes one organisation different from another. The culture within an organisation may be one of team work – where everyone helps each other to ensure all tasks are completed on time and appropriately by the team as a whole, or one of each member of staff keeping to their own roles and responsibilities. There may be a culture of control, where all rules and procedures are adhered to at all times, or one that is more relaxed where controls are more informal and trust is an important part of the controls in place.

One way to illustrate this is to consider how a new driver might have to drive to pass their driving test, with the examiner sat next to them in the car, and then to consider how they may drive 15 years later. Both would be safe, and keeping within certain rules, but the driving itself might be quite different!

No one culture is right or wrong and different styles of management will be appropriate for different types of organisation.

Management styles

The style of management in organisations directly affects how the organisation operates, and therefore its culture. The main styles of management are:

Democratic – a democratic manager delegates authority to his or her staff. The manager gives them complete responsibility to complete tasks using their own work methods, but within certain organisation boundaries. This is also known as empowerment of staff. A democratic manager will also involve employees in decision making and this can be motivating. It can however lead to slower decision making as all staff are consulted first.

BPP
LEARNING MEDIA

Autocratic – an autocratic manager will dictate orders to staff and make all decisions without consultation with them. Therefore decision making is quick, but staff are not consulted which can de-motivate them. They are not empowered and can feel undervalued.

Consultative – a consultative manager is one with a combination of the democratic and autocratic management styles. Views and opinions will be asked for from staff before decisions are made but the ultimate decision making still lies with the manager.

Laissez faire – a laissez faire manager will set their staff a task and then give them complete freedom to complete it in any way they like. The manager will be there to answer questions and to perhaps counsel and coach staff to complete the work, but will not be involved in actually doing it. Staff can be motivated by this but can also feel that they lack guidance and do not reach the goals set.

It should be noted that no one management style is right or wrong. Which style is right for an organisation depends on the factors below and on the subordinate styles of the staff working within the organisation.

Other factors affecting culture

Culture will depend on many factors, not just management style. In this unit you will need to briefly consider the management style and culture in place in your chosen organisation and whether it is appropriate to it. In doing this you will have to think carefully about the organisation and the factors that influence the culture within the accounts department, and whether it is appropriate to the organisation or not.

Factors affecting an organisations culture might include:

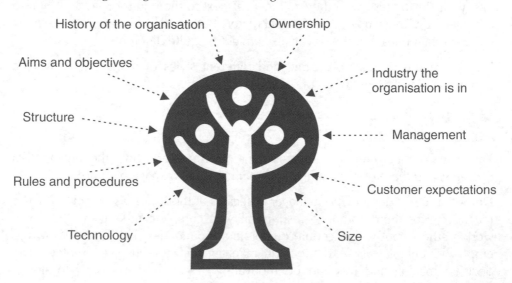

Stakeholders to the accounts department

There are many internal stakeholders in an organisation that may be reliant on the information the accounts department produces, in order that they can carry out their own function for the organisation both effectively and efficiently.

Task 3

Read through the sample Case Study at the back of this workbook. This is the Case Study published by the AAT as an example of what you will be provided with if you are unable to complete this unit based on your own organisation.

The Case Study provides you with information on a fictitious organisation. In order to write your final report you will need to imagine you work for that organisation, that the scenario is real, and consists of the knowledge you have built up by working there.

Who are the stakeholders in the accounts department of Cookridge and Cookridge Carpets Limited and what are their information needs – both financial and management?

Think of stakeholders that may be mentioned specifically by the scenario and also general ones that would exist within any typical organisation.

Are there any information needs that are not currently being met? What additional information could be produced to ensure decision makers are better informed?

REPORT

When completing this section of your report you will need to research the information your organisation's accounts department produces, both for external and internal use. You will also need to research how your accounts department is organised and structured and perhaps include an organisation chart in an appendix.

As part of your accounts department section you should briefly explain where the accounting department of the organisation is based and whether it is centralised, decentralised or outsourced. You should also include how the accounts department communicates with other parts of the organisation.

You will need to review whether financial and management reports are adequate and whether information needs of decision makers are being adequately met. You could do this by completing an analysis of internal stakeholders to the accounts department and reviewing their information needs. From this review you will be expected to make recommendations as to how to improve the organisation's accounting systems. Chapter 4 contains more advice on how to complete this.

Checklist

- Review the organisation's accounts department structure and how it communicates with other parts of the organisation.

- Review the internal stakeholders to the accounts department.

- Review what financial and management accounting reports are being produced.

- Review whether information needs are being met.

- Research critical incidents that may have occurred because information needs have not been met.

- Include diagrams such as organisation charts of the accounts department in the appendices.

- Write short, individually numbered paragraphs.

- Write only in the third person.

- Make recommendations to improve information needs not currently being met (you may put this in a separate recommendations section if you wish).

Case Study Advice

When you have read the Case Study through you will notice some areas of the required research outlined above are clearly mentioned and some are not. Consider the Case Study to be a story about an organisation, so areas not covered perhaps do not feature in the organisation at present. For example you may need to construct an organisation chart of the accounts team in order that you can fully analyse its structure and complete a review of critical incidents so that you can review whether information needs are met.

You may also need to assume whether basic financial and management reports are being produced and whether they are being used by key decision makers. In the sample report in the back of this workbook we have assumed that not many reports are currently being produced by the accounts team. This is because the system is decentralised and there does not appear to be evidence that the decision makers are using them. The owners seem to regularly be surprised by the lack of funds in the bank for example.

Immerse yourself in the scenario and remember that the report must read in the same way as if it were your actual workplace. Use your skills, knowledge and imagination to supplement the case scenario and to make a detailed analysis of the situation, and to make recommendations to improve, clearly explaining the benefit to the organisation.

The sample report at the back of this workbook will aid your understanding as to how to complete this. Remember to send your draft to your assessor for review –

it will aid their authentication of your work and provide you with valuable feedback on your progress.

FAQS

1   **How do I research the structure of my accounts department?** – You should look at the documentation your organisation produces, often found on organisation intranets, or interview your accounts managers and draw up an organisation chart yourself. This will help you understand the current structure of the department, and whether it meets the organisation's needs.

2   **I work in a large organisation with several large sections to the accounts department, how do I include this in my report?** – Within your report you can include brief detail explaining the overall size and structure of your accounts department, and how the organisation ensures it does (or does not!) communicate with other parts of the business. You will see in Chapter 4 that as you start the detailed research on the weaknesses within the accounts system that you can then focus this research on just one part of the system, rather than the department as a whole.

3   **Where do I include the results of this research in my report?** – This chapter can be included as one section in your report – the accounts department. It can include basic, brief, information about the accounts department and its stakeholders. It will also include a brief description as to how the accounts system is structured. This is to set the scene for the reader so that they better understand the context of the main review completed in the next section. In the internal stakeholder analysis you can include detail of information needs not met, based around your research of the system and the information it produces plus critical incidents that have occurred. There will be more guidance on how to do this in Chapter 4 so it may be helpful to work through that chapter first.

4   **How do I review critical incidents in my workplace to understand if information needs have been met?** – A good place to start would be to interview management and staff who work as part of the accounts team. Also to review any recent reports such as internal audit reports on the work of the department or team. Remember that the reason you are completing this research is to understand where information needs are not being met. As part of your interviews you could include this question for key decision makers to see what information they would like that they are currently not receiving.

5   **My organisation/manager is concerned about the confidentiality of what I put in my report** – First of all you should note that this report is looking at the organisation, its accounting systems and information and making recommendations to improve them. This should benefit the organisation. You are putting this information into a professional management report and

submitting it to your assessor for assessment. The work is confidential and your assessor will not be reproducing it or sharing it with other students. To complete this report you do not need to share critical or sensitive information and your assessor will be able to advise you if management have concerns about certain aspects of your report. You must accept though that at the end of the report your assessor will require a statement, from you manager and on company headed paper, that the work is your own, unaided and a true reflection of the organisation. If your manager or supervisor is unwilling to provide this then you must not complete the work on your workplace, but on an AAT Case Study instead.

6   **What Financial and Management Accounting Reports do I need to include in my research?** – Try and research as many reports as necessary that are produced by the accounts department. You are not required to complete a detailed report on each, or even include them all in the appendices. You should ensure that you at least cover the main financial accounting reports – the statement of profit or loss , the statement of cash flows and the statement of financial position. Try to also include management accounting reports.

chapter 4:
ACCOUNTING SYSTEMS

chapter coverage 📖

In this chapter we will look at some examples of how accounting systems might be structured and consider how they provide information to key stakeholders of the organisation.

We will then consider how to assess whether the accounting systems in place are suitable for the organisation and whether any improvements could be made to them.

Following on from that we will introduce the importance of controls within accounting departments and systems. We will look at the role controls play and consider examples of basic controls that should be in place. Within this section we will look at the importance of procedures and documentation, as a control tool, but also as a support to the individuals who use the accounting systems.

An example of documentation we will consider in more detail is the mapping of accounting systems and workflow. This can be completed by constructing diagrams such as flowcharts and we will look at the value and purpose of these.

We will then consider how to identify weaknesses in accounting systems – looking at tools to assist us with this such as a SWOT and/or PEST analysis. We will then consider recommendations to improve the systems and address weaknesses identified.

Next, we look at how to ensure ethics are taken in to account in accounting systems, particularly the five fundamental principles of the AAT Code of Professional Ethics.

Sustainability is also a key issue for organisations. We consider how to review the accounting system against sustainability principles, considering social, corporate and environmental factors.

Finally we will explain how to write up this part of the report and include tips for those using a Case Study scenario.

LEARNING OUTCOMES

1.4 – Explain how the accounting systems are affected by the organisational structure, systems, procedures and business transactions

2.5 – Explain how an internal control system can support the accounting function

3.1 – Identify an organisation's accounting system requirements including hardware and software packages

3.2 – Review record keeping systems to confirm whether they meet an organisation's requirements

3.3 – Identify weaknesses in, and the potential for improvements to, the accounting system and consider the impact on the operation of an organisation

3.5 – Review methods of operating for cost effectiveness, reliability and speed

4.1 – Evaluate the accounting system against ethical principles

4.2 – Identify actual or possible breaches of professional ethics

5.1 – Evaluate the accounting system against sustainable principles

5.2 – Identify where improvements could be made to improve sustainability

6.2 – Identify the effects that any recommended changes would have on the users of the system

6.3 – Enable individuals to understand how to use the accounting system by use of:

- Training
- Manuals
- Written information
- Help menus

ACCOUNTING SYSTEMS

A system is any function that takes an input, processes it, and then produces an output. An ACCOUNTING SYSTEM is a system that takes raw data as its input, processes this, and then produces many outputs as discussed in Chapter 3.

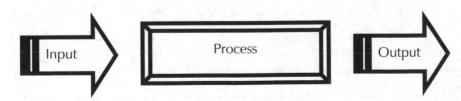

Input → Process → Output

BPP
LEARNING MEDIA

The aim of any accounting system is to fully support the accounting team to process accurately and fully all accounting transactions so that financial and management information provided to stakeholders is accurate and complete.

If an accounting system within an organisation is not effective in completing this objective then the accounting information may be incorrect and not available to stakeholders when key decisions need to be made.

There are many different types of computerised accounting systems that exist within organisations. An accounting system consists of many different inputs, processes and outputs and that systems can be both computerised and manual. Either or both may be appropriate to your organisation and to complete this section of your report you will be expected to analyse your chosen system, map its processes, analyse its strengths and weaknesses and then make recommendations to improve it.

Accounting systems within organisations can be centralised or decentralised. The definitions of these are very similar to those for the department itself as discussed in Chapter 3. A **centralised** accounting system is one where all the data is stored at a central location, and accounts staff process it centrally, although this may be by accessing the system from many different locations.

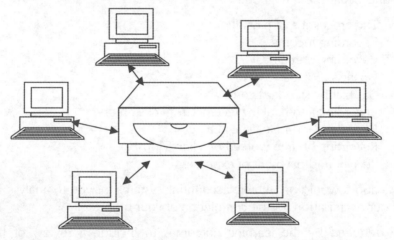

A centralised accounting system

A **decentralised** system is one where the data is stored and processed separately, perhaps independently by staff at different locations or with different computers. There is no link between processes, each being formed independently of each other.

Task 1

What are the advantages of a centralised system?

What advantages would a decentralised system have?

Which do you think would be more appropriate to Cookridge and Cookridge Carpets Ltd as featured in the example Case Study at the back of this workbook?

List out the advantages of both types of system and then read back through the Case Study and think about what type of system is more appropriate to Cookridge and Cookridge Carpets Ltd and why. Consider what information the key stakeholders in Cookridge and Cookridge Carpets Ltd need and whether these information needs are met by the current system. Review our suggested answers at the back of this workbook when you have completed this task.

Examples of accounting systems

As already mentioned, a system is any activity that takes an input and processes it into an output. This can be computerised or manual. Examples of systems within an accounts department might be:

- The processing of payroll
- Recording income
- Recording purchases
- Paying suppliers
- Calculating standard costs
- Recording and banking receipts from customers
- Recording and managing petty cash
- Recording of time worked on clients/jobs
- Receipt and payment of expenses

All of the above would be suitable accounting systems for you to analyse in detail within your organisation for the completion of your report.

You are required by the learning outcomes to include a review of how the accounting systems in your organisation are structured, and whether they are appropriate to it and then to complete a more detailed analysis of one part of the system in particular, mapping how it currently operates and analysing any strengths and/or weaknesses within it. From this you are then expected to make recommendations to improve the accounting system.

The system you choose to analyse in detail can be your own role at work or the work of your department of team. It could also be one part of your role – especially if you work in a small team where you each take on several processes or functions.

BPP LEARNING MEDIA

For example, you could investigate the purchase ledger function in your organisation, or the credit control or payroll function.

Whichever you choose it should be of sufficient value to the organisation (petty cash or expenses would not be sufficient unless they account for a large amount of expenditure in the organisation and take up a significant amount of the time of the accounting team).

The system you choose should ideally also be analysed with reference to appropriate controls, which will be a later section in your report.

If you are unsure as to what to do you should discuss this with your assessor and include your approach in your project proposal to ensure you receive appropriate feedback and support.

It may be helpful when doing this to consider yourself to be a consultant in the work place.

SYSTEM CONTROLS

All of the systems in place, in any department of any organisation, must be controlled in order that they operate safely, efficiently and effectively. Controls can include computerised controls (such as passwords or restrictions on staff performing certain operations) or manual (such as internal audit reviews and supervisory checks).

Accounting systems often have controls built into them to ensure they meet certain regulations and or requirements and then have formal reviews of these controls by auditors and or management to ensure they are appropriate and effective.

Internal controls are discussed in more detail in Chapter 5 where we look at specific examples of controls and the role of the internal auditing team. For this section we will address the importance of controls within accounting systems in general.

Controls are required because systems need to adapt and change, as the internal and/or external environment changes. They also ensure that the system continues to operate safely. In the concept of accounting systems they therefore ensure that the system is keeping within the regulatory framework and the rules and procedures of the organisation.

Specific controls will be discussed in more detail in the next chapter but for now we will consider one control in particular – that of documenting the accounting system including the procedures and/or user manuals for those that operate it.

> ## Task 2
>
> What are the advantages of an accounts department having a full user manual for all activities that take place within it?
>
> What might the disadvantages of such an approach be?
>
> Write down as many advantages and disadvantages as you can before reviewing the suggested answers.

Producing adequate documentation to map an accounting system, and provide manuals to assist users, is an intensive process, and such documents can quickly become out of date if the system is subject to change. It will, however, ensure that the way in which the system is required to operate is set out for users and will assist them in making sure the information output from the system is on time and of the correct quality.

Other important controls to consider within the accounting system itself are passwords and access controls. Accounting systems are complex and in any size of organisation it can be possible to restrict access to the system so that only staff that need access to particular functions are provided with it.

This can be completed in two ways. Firstly a system of passwords can be set up so that different parts of the system require different passwords to access. Staff can then only be provided with access to the parts of the system required.

Systems also often have administrator access where nominated administrators can set up access, but only to specific sections of the system. For example so that a accounts payable (purchase ledger) clerk cannot access the accounts receivable (sales ledger) or payroll functions. These are important controls so that staff can not complete operations that are not related to their role. It also aids the division of responsibilities so that certain key staff can not perform all the activities necessary to carry out fraud.

For example, if an accounts payable clerk is able to raise a purchase order, book goods into inventory and then process an invoice, they may be able to purchase goods for their own use, and then process the payment through the organisation's system. By not allowing the same member of staff access to all three of these activities the risk of fraud is significantly reduced.

When passwords are used by staff there should also be controls set in place regarding their use and control.

Task 3

Imagine you are the manager of an accounts department and are in the process of implementing a new accounting system.

All staff are being provided with their own passwords to access the parts of the system necessary to perform their work.

What rules would you put in place regarding the use and controls of passwords? Why are these important?

You will find this task easier if you think about the possible consequences of poor controls on passwords. Review the suggested answer once you have done so.

ANALYSING SYSTEMS

System flowchart

As already mentioned, all processes consist of a series of inputs that are processed into outputs. In a payroll process the input will be the staff hours worked, pay scales etc. The process would be to calculate the payroll and the output would be that the staff are paid. Each stage of this process can be analysed in detail and it may be helpful to **draw a system flowchart**. This shows the key decision making processes, inputs and outputs and can be included in the appendices to your report.

There are many ways of drawing a flowchart with symbols to show each stage of the process. Although these methods are appropriate, and can be used if you have studied them in the past, a simple flow chart can also be used that clearly shows the flow of the system using boxes and text.

For example:

Reading through the sample Case Study at the back of this workbook it is relatively straightforward to complete a simple system flowchart of the payroll system. An appropriate one could be:

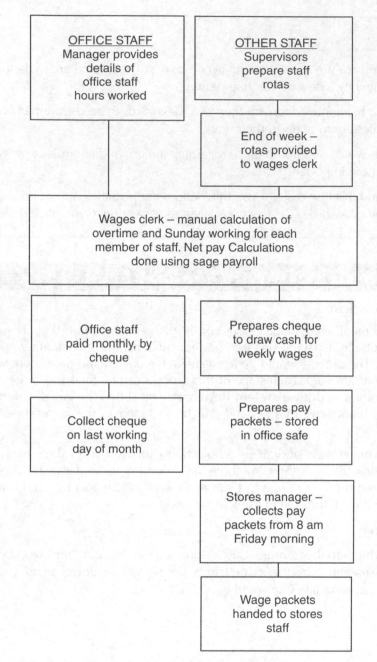

The above flowchart reflects our interpretation of the information provided in the Case Study scenario. When completing a system flowchart your are aiming to map out the system process as accurately as possible. If you are working from a case study then you may find that not all the information required is available. For example, the flowchart set out above assumes that the manager must provide details of office staff working hours. This is not explicit in the scenario itself.

By completing a system flowchart and mapping a process in detail, you should start to identify some improvements which can be made to the system and to the organisation. It is a requirement of this unit that appropriate recommendations be made to improve your selected system.

Task 4

Complete a system flowchart for the accounts payable function using the sample Case Study information at the back of this workbook.

Having completed this, and also by reviewing the example flowchart for the payroll process – what recommendations can you think of to improve these systems for the organisation?

SWOT analysis

Another tool to aid you to analyse the system in detail is a SWOT analysis. SWOT stands for:

Strengths
Weaknesses
Opportunities
Threats

The **Strengths** and **Weaknesses** to a system will be internal factors that either make it particularly effective or demonstrate clear weaknesses within it.

An example strength may be that a payroll system is operated by knowledgeable and experienced staff and a weakness might be that is a manual process, dependent on manual calculation which presents many opportunities for human error.

Once strengths and weaknesses have been identified then recommendations can be considered to address the weaknesses.

Opportunities and **Threats** are external to the actual system itself. There may be an opportunity to train more staff in payroll qualifications. A threat would be that information and legislation relating to payroll is subject to frequent change (tax codes, tax rates, NI contributions etc).

It is sometimes harder to identify external factors such as these but you should try and consider as many as you can – they will also help you to identify recommendations to improve the system.

Task 5

Read through the sample Case Study provided at the back of this workbook. Complete a SWOT analysis as below, focusing on the strengths and weaknesses of the internal accounting systems, and the opportunities and threats on the organisation as a whole.

Strengths

Weaknesses

Opportunities

Threats

Once you have completed this, review our suggested answer. Did you come up with similar Strengths, Weaknesses, Opportunities and Threats? Sometimes answers can be down to interpretation, especially between Strengths and Opportunities and Weaknesses and Threats. Do not worry about which heading you listed each under, it is enough that you identified them.

In the section of your report that completes the analysis of an accounting system you should include a summary of your SWOT analysis, particularly the weaknesses identified. The SWOT analysis itself should be placed in the report's appendices, with reference to it within the summary.

BPP
LEARNING MEDIA

PEST analysis

A final tool that may assist you in analysing your chosen system is a PEST analysis. A PEST analysis investigates four factors that may affect your organisation and the system. These four factors are:

Political
Economic
Social
Technological

Political factors – There are a variety of political factors that can affect the operation of an accounting system. These might include the following:

- Changes in NIC rates
- Changes in VAT rates
- Changes in company legislation regarding publication of financial statements
- Changes in financial reporting standards

Economic factors – Examples of economic factors that might affect the accounting system are:

- Increase/decrease in the volume of transactions due to general or specific changes in the economy and customer demands
- Changes in the availability and wage rate of the labour force
- The staff available to work in the accounting function
- The budget applied to the accounting function

General or specific economic changes may lead to an increase or decrease in the general level of transactions of an organisation. This will have a direct effect on the number of transactions within an accounting function although not necessarily on the nature of those transactions or the method of operations.

Social factors – Social factors that might affect the accounting system could include the following:

- Changing work patterns such as flexitime and home working
- Family commitments leading to changes such as part time working and job sharing
- Employment legislation

Technological factors – Examples of technological factors that might cause changes in the accounts system might be:

- Advances in computer technology
- Security issues
- Technological fraud
- On-line banking

In the section of your report that contains the analysis of an accounting system include a summary of your PEST analysis and make reference to it in the appendices.

You should now have completed enough research into the chosen accounting system to be able to make some recommendations for improvement.

Remember that your recommendations do not have to be implemented – the purpose of your report is to investigate and analyse and then to make recommendations to improve – it would be unusual if all recommendations were implemented.

The **learning outcomes** for this unit require you to make your recommendations clear and easily understood and to support them with a clear rationale as to why they are appropriate. In order to demonstrate competence in this area you are required to fully justify **all** your recommendations, plus explain them in summary format in an Executive Summary (more on this in Chapter 7).

ETHICS

Ethics are a set of moral principles that guide behaviour.

Ethical values are assumptions and beliefs about what constitutes 'right' and 'wrong' behaviour.

Individuals have ethical values, often reflecting the beliefs of the families, cultures and educational environments in which they developed their ideas.

Organisations also have ethical values, based on the norms and standards of behaviour that their leaders believe will best help them express their identity and achieve their objectives.

The concept of **business ethics** suggests that businesses are morally responsible for their actions, and should be held accountable for the effects of their actions on people and society. This is true for individual businesses (which should behave ethically towards the employees, customers, suppliers and communities who are affected by them) and for 'business' in general, which has a duty to behave responsibly in the interests of the society of which it is a part.

FUNDAMENTAL ETHICAL PRINCIPLES

The AAT has a **Code of Professional Ethics** (the AAT Code) which sets out five **fundamental principles** that underpin ethical behaviour in an accounting context:

Fundamental principle	Explanation	Section of AAT Code
Integrity	A member shall be straightforward and honest in all professional and business relationships.	110
Objectivity	A member shall not allow bias, conflict of interest or undue influence of others to override professional or business relationships.	120
Professional competence and due care	A member has a continuing duty to maintain professional knowledge and skill at the level required to ensure that a client or employer receives competent professional service based on current developments in practice, legislation and techniques. A member shall act diligently and in accordance with applicable and professional standards when providing professional services.	130
Confidentiality	A member shall, in accordance with the law, respect the confidentiality of information acquired as a result of professional and business relationships and not disclose any such information to third parties without proper and specific authority unless there is a legal or professional right or duty to disclose. Confidential information acquired as a result of professional and business relationships shall not be used for the personal advantage of the member or third parties.	140
Professional behaviour	A member shall comply with relevant laws and regulations and avoid any action that brings the profession into disrepute.	150

Let's look at each of these in turn.

Integrity – section 110

110.1 'The principle of **integrity** imposes an obligation on all members to be straightforward and honest in professional and business relationships. Integrity also implies fair dealing and truthfulness.

110.2 A member shall not be associated with reports, returns, communications or other information where they believe that the information:

(i)   Contains a false or misleading statement

(ii)   Contains statements or information furnished recklessly

(iii)   Omits or obscures information required to be included where such omission or obscurity would be misleading.'

On an everyday level, integrity involves matters such as being **open** about the limitations of your knowledge or competence, being **honest** in your relationships and carrying out your work **accurately, conscientiously and efficiently**.

Objectivity – section 120

120.1 'The principle of objectivity imposes an obligation on all members not to compromise their professional or business judgement because of bias, conflict of interest or the undue influence of others.'

This is a very important principle for the accounting profession because it protects the interests both of the parties directly affected by an accountant's services and of the general public (who rely on the accuracy of information and the integrity of financial systems).

Objectivity is the principle that all professional and business judgements should be made fairly:

- On the basis of an **independent** and intellectually honest appraisal of information

- **Free from** all forms of **prejudice** and **bias**

- Free from factors which might affect **impartiality**, such as pressure from a superior, financial interest in the outcome, a personal or professional relationship with one of the parties involved, or a conflict of interest (where one client stands to lose and another to gain by a particular disclosure)

Task 6

A member who is straightforward and honest in all business and professional relationships can be said to be following the fundamental principle of objectivity.

	✓
True	
False	

Professional competence and due care – section 130

Accountants have an obligation to their employers and clients to know what they are doing – and to do it right! The following is taken from the AAT Code:

130.1 'The principle of **professional competence** and due care imposes the following obligations on members:

   (i)   To maintain **professional knowledge** and **skill** at the level required to ensure that clients or employers receive competent professional service and

   (ii)   To **act diligently** in accordance with applicable technical and professional standards when providing professional services

130.2 Competent professional service requires the exercise of **sound judgement** in applying professional knowledge and skill in the performance of such service. Professional competence may be divided into two separate phases:

   (i)   Attainment of professional competence

   (ii)   Maintenance of professional competence

130.3 The **maintenance of professional competence** requires continuing awareness and understanding of relevant technical, professional and business developments. Continuing professional development (CPD) develops and maintains the capabilities that enable a member to perform competently within the professional environment. To achieve this, Council expects all members to undertake CPD in accordance with the AAT *Policy on continuing professional development*. This requires members to assess, plan, action and evaluate their learning and development needs.

130.4 **Diligence** encompasses the **responsibility** to act in accordance with the requirements of an assignment, carefully, thoroughly and on a timely basis.

130.5 A member shall take reasonable steps to ensure that those working under the member's authority in a **professional capacity** have appropriate **training** and **supervision**.

130.6 Where appropriate, a member shall make clients, employers or other users of the professional services aware of **limitations** inherent in the services to avoid the misinterpretation of an expression of opinion as an assertion of fact.'

You should understand from this that you must not agree to carry out a task or assignment if you do not have the competence to carry it out to a **satisfactory standard** – unless you are sure that you will be able to get the help and advice you need to do so. And if you discover in the course of performing a task or assignment that you lack the knowledge or competence to complete it satisfactorily, you should not continue without taking steps to get the help you need.

In addition, once you have become a member of the profession, you need to maintain and develop your professional and **technical competence**, to keep pace with the demands which may be made on you in your work – and developments which may affect your work over time. This may mean:

- Regularly reviewing your practices against national and international standards, codes, regulations and legislation. Are you complying with the latest requirements?

- Continually upgrading your knowledge and skills in line with developments in accounting practices, requirements and techniques – and making sure that you do not get 'rusty' in the skills you have!

Due care is a legal concept that means that, having agreed to do a task or assignment, you have an obligation to carry it out to the best of your ability, in the client's or employer's best interests, within reasonable timescales and with proper regard for the technical and professional standards expected of you as a professional.

As the expert in your field, you may often deal with others who have little knowledge of accounting matters. This puts you in a position of power, which must never be abused by carrying out your task or assignment in a negligent or 'careless' way.

References and professional liability

Accountants in practice may be asked by clients or third parties to **provide references**. For example, to provide a reference to a client's bank in support of the client's mortgage application.

The main danger in giving such references is that the accountant may be sued for **damages** if the reference proves to be **unreasonable** or **incorrect.** In order to avoid liability, the accountant must be able to prove that they acted as a reasonable professional accountant would have. This means that the accountant must be **professionally competent** to make the reference and exercise **due care** in doing so. If they provide the reference in absence of full knowledge of the facts, or without exercising due care, then they risk being found liable for damages.

To safeguard against the risk of being sued for damages, accountants may add a **disclaimer of liability** to their work.

Examples of such a disclaimer include:

'Whilst every care has been taken in the preparation of this document, it may contain errors for which we cannot be responsible.'

or

'This report is prepared for the use of X (the client) only. No responsibility is assumed to any other person.'

The **effectiveness** of such disclaimers is **open to question** by the court. A disclaimer is unlikely to protect the accountant that makes a reckless or negligent statement. It may also **devalue** the report or reference since it gives the impression that the accountant is not confident in the work they have done.

Confidentiality – section 140

140.1 The principle of **confidentiality** imposes an obligation on members to refrain from:

(i) **Disclosing** outside the firm or employing organisation confidential information acquired as a result of professional and business relationships without proper and specific authority or unless there is a legal or professional right or duty to disclose.

(ii) **Using confidential information** acquired as a result of professional and business relationships to their personal advantage or the advantage of third parties.

Information about a past, present, or prospective client's or **employer's affairs**, or the affairs of clients of employers, acquired in a work context, is likely to be confidential if it is not a matter of public knowledge.

140.2 A member shall maintain confidentiality even in a **social environment.** The member shall be alert to the possibility of inadvertent disclosure, particularly in circumstances involving close or personal relations, associates and long established business relationships.

140.3 A member shall maintain confidentiality of information disclosed by a **prospective client** or **employer**.

140.4 A member shall maintain confidentiality of information within the firm or **employing organisation**.

140.5 A member shall take all **reasonable steps** to ensure that **staff under their control** and persons from whom advice and assistance is obtained **respect** the principle of **confidentiality**. The restriction on using confidential information also means not using it for any purpose other than that for which it was legitimately acquired.

140.6 The need to comply with the principle of confidentiality **continues even after the end of relationships** between a member and a client or employer. When a member changes employment or acquires a new client, the member is entitled to use prior experience. The member shall not, however, use or disclose any confidential information either acquired or received as a result of a professional or business relationship.'

Confidentiality is a very important fundamental principle but there are circumstances where the law **allows or requires** that confidentiality to be breached. These circumstances are described in the AAT Code in section 140.7 and are summarised in the table below.

Circumstances	Examples
Disclosure is permitted by law and is authorised by the client or employer.	Providing working papers to a new firm who is taking on the client
Disclosure is required by law.	Providing documents or other evidence for legal proceedings
	Disclosure to HMRC
	Disclosure of actual/suspected money laundering or terrorist financing to the firm's Money Laundering Reporting Officer (MLRO) or to the Serious Organised Crime Agency (SOCA) (in the UK)
There is a professional right or duty to disclose which is in the public interest and is not prohibited by law.	Complying with the quality review of an IFAC member body or other professional body
	Responding to an inquiry or investigation by the AAT or other regulatory or professional body
	Disclosure to protect the member's professional interests in legal proceedings
	A disclosure made to comply with technical standards and ethics requirements

It is vital to appreciate the importance of the fundamental principle of **confidentiality**. You need to respect the confidentiality of information acquired as a result of professional and business relationships. This means that you will not use or disclose confidential information to others, unless:

- You have **specific** and **'proper' authorisation** to do so by the client or employer.

- You are legally or professionally **entitled** or **obliged** to do so.

It is also worth being aware that personal information shared with you by clients and colleagues at work should be regarded as confidential – unless you are told otherwise: this is an important basis for trust in any working relationship.

Task 7

In which of the following circumstances do you have a legal duty to disclose confidential information concerning a customer of your organisation?

	✓
If they are asked for during legal proceedings	
When your manager tells you to disclose the information	
When writing a report for general circulation within your organisation	

Professional behaviour – section 150

The final fundamental principle is professional behaviour. On this principle the AAT Code states:

150.1 'The principle of **professional behaviour** imposes an obligation on members to comply with relevant laws and regulations and avoid any action that may bring disrepute to the profession. This includes actions which a **reasonable and informed third party**, having knowledge of all relevant information, would conclude negatively affect the good reputation of the profession.

Members should note that conduct reflecting adversely on the reputation of the AAT is a ground for disciplinary action under the AAT's *Disciplinary Regulations*.'

An example is when advertising their services, members must ensure that they are honest and truthful. They can bring the profession into disrepute by making **exaggerated claims** about services, their qualifications and experience, or if they make **disparaging references or unsubstantiated comparisons** to the work of others.

Applying this principle means **'being professional'**. You'll have your own ideas about what 'being professional' means, but in a sense, it involves complying with the law and behaving in a way that maintains or enhances the reputation of your profession: bringing it credit – not discredit.

One key aspect of this is **courtesy**. As a professional, you should behave with courtesy and consideration towards anyone you come into contact with in the course of your work and indeed in your personal life.

> **These fundamental principles are very IMPORTANT! You MUST understand and be able to recognise and apply each of them.**

IDENTIFYING ETHICAL ISSUES

Now that we've considered the fundamental principles in general, let's consider some typical scenarios in which they might be helpful. In each case, we will identify the ethical issues they present, in line with the basic principles discussed so far. For the purposes of these questions you should assume you are an AAT student.

Incident one

You are asked to produce an aged receivables' listing for your manager as soon as possible. However you do not have up to date figures because of a problem with the computer system. A colleague suggests that to get the report done in time you use averages for the missing figures.

There is an **integrity** issue here. Using averages instead of actual figures will almost certainly result in an inaccurate listing. You should report the problem to your manager and ask for an extension to your deadline in order to provide an accurate listing.

Incident two

You have received a letter from an estate agent, requesting financial information about one of your company's customers that is applying to rent a property. The information is needed as soon as possible, by fax or e-mail, in order to secure approval for the rent agreement.

There is a **confidentiality** issue here. You need the customer's authority to disclose the information; you may also need to confirm the identity of the person making the request. You should also take steps to protect the confidentiality of the information when you send it: for example, not using fax or e-mail (which can be intercepted), and stating clearly that the information is confidential.

Incident three

While out to lunch, you run into a friend at the sandwich bar. In conversation, she tells you that she expects to inherit from a recently deceased uncle, and asks you how she will be affected by inheritance tax, capital gains tax and other matters.

There are issues of **professional competence and due care** here. You are not qualified to give advice on matters of taxation. Even if you were qualified, any answer you give on the spot would risk being incomplete or inaccurate with potentially serious consequences.

Incident four

A client of the accountancy practice you work in is so pleased with the service you gave him this year that he offers you a free weekend break in a luxury hotel, just as a 'thank you'.

There is an **objectivity** issue here as the gift is of significant value. Think about how it looks: a third party observer is entitled to wonder what 'special favours' deserve this extra reward – and/or how such a gift may bias you in the client's favour in future.

Task 8

Read through the sample Case Study provided at the back of this workbook. Complete a review of ethics within the accounting system, focusing on the five fundamental principles (integrity, objectivity, professional competence and due care, confidentiality and professional behaviour).

You should include details of any breach, or potential breach, of the five principles that you have identified; explain which principle the actions breach, and recommend alternative action that should be taken to prevent the breach occurring.

SUSTAINABILITY

Accountants are expected to act in the public interest, and in the modern business world, the concepts of **sustainability** and **corporate social responsibility** are increasingly important in this regard.

Sustainability

Sustainability is concerned with ensuring activities can continue indefinitely without damaging the environment. *Goldsmith and Samson (2004)* define sustainability as 'a long-term programme involving a series of sustainable development practices, aimed at improving organisational efficiency, stakeholder support and market edge.'

Sustainable development is a core part of an organisation's corporate social responsibility (see below) and as the above definition suggests, it comprises efficiency, stakeholder support and market edge.

Policies aimed at improving **efficiency** include reducing waste, using less energy and recycling. **Stakeholder support** can be gained through practices such as encouraging flexible working, cycle-to-work schemes, reducing business travel through the use of technology and sourcing materials from green suppliers. Examples of **market edge** policies are research and development, supply chain improvements and innovation.

Another definition of sustainability can be found in the **UN's Brundtland Report**. According to this, organisations must aim to 'meet the needs of the present without compromising the ability of future generations to meet their own needs.'

Corporate social responsibility

The concept of corporate social responsibility (CSR) was established by the expectation in society that **companies are accountable** for the social and ethical effects of their actions.

A company's CSR can be defined as the **obligations** that it feels that it has to the community, persons and organisations connected to it and to society as a whole. For example, organisations that source materials from developing countries may feel they should ensure workers involved in the production of those materials are treated fairly.

As accountants play a **central role** in the operation of a business, they are key to the organisation upholding these values.

DUTIES AND RESPONSIBILITIES OF FINANCE PROFESSIONALS IN RELATION TO SUSTAINABILITY

The definition of sustainability from the **UN's Brundtland Report** makes it clear that business organisations have a duty to **protect society** and **future generations**, and as part of the business world, finance professionals have a duty to consider the economic, social and environmental aspects of their work in order to support sustainability.

Duties of finance professionals

The diagram below shows how economic, social and environmental issues are linked.

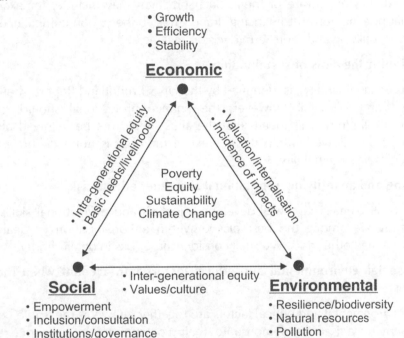

Economic aspects that finance professionals may consider include, supporting their organisation or clients to be profitable, supporting local businesses when deciding on suppliers and paying them on time and looking for ways to improve the efficiency of the organisation's finance operations.

Social aspects may include supporting policies on corporate governance and consulting the local community when making decisions on investing in or relocating operations.

Environment aspects are usually in relation to using less energy and creating less pollution. A finance professional should therefore support company policies on the long-term management of resources and facilitating the running of their

organisation in a sustainable manner. These may include, for example, not printing emails unless necessary, turning lights off at the end of the day and recycling materials used in their office.

Responsibilities of finance professionals

There are six main responsibilities of finance professionals in regards to upholding the principles of sustainability.

Creating and promoting an ethical culture

Finance professionals should help senior management create and promote an ethical culture within their organisation. Primarily it means supporting ethical policies as they are introduced, but it also means discouraging illegal or unethical practices if they are aware of them. Such practices may include, for example, money laundering, terrorist financing, fraud, theft, bribery, non-compliance with regulations, bullying and short-term decision making.

Championing the aims of sustainability

The aims of sustainability, as identified by the UN's Brundtland Report, should be promoted and followed. However, the finance professional should remain objective at all times. This means that the aims should not be followed blindly, but instead be followed within the context of the organisation's culture and its own policies on sustainability.

Evaluating and quantifying reputational and other ethical risks

Finance professionals have well-developed analysis and evaluational skills. This means they are among the best placed within an organisation to deal with reputational and other risks. We shall consider these risks in detail shortly.

Taking social, environmental and ethical factors into account when making decisions

Social, environmental and ethical factors are together known as the 'triple bottom line'. Many organisations demonstrate their commitment to corporate social responsibility (CSR) by including in their financial reports, organisational performance information based on these factors. Financial professionals have a responsibility to take these factors into account when making decisions so that when organisational position and performance is measured, the business can clearly demonstrate its commitment to CSR.

Promoting sustainable practices

As well as promoting policies in relation to ethical and illegal practices, finance professionals should also support sustainability practices developed by the organisation. Such practices may be in relation to, for example, products and services, customers, employees, the workplace, supply chain and business functions and processes.

Raising awareness of social responsibility

As mentioned earlier, finance professionals should consider the sustainability impacts of their decisions and actions. By doing so, they will help raise awareness of sustainability within the organisation as colleagues, who may be in different departments, see them taking a lead in this area.

Task 9

Think of some examples of sustainability and corporate social responsibility issues in the place that you work.

REPORT

When completing this section of your report you will firstly need to decide which part of the accounting system you are going to review, and make recommendations to improve. Depending on the size of your organisation you may choose to analyse the whole system, or just one part of it. Your assessor should be able to advise you on this. You will then need to conduct a complete review of the part of the accounting system you have chosen.

An effective way to start this would be to first complete a SWOT analysis. The SWOT analysis itself would be included as one of the appendices of the report. You would then summarise the outcomes of this in the report itself.

The AAT suggest that in order to do this you break this section of your report into several smaller sections:

- Working methods and practices
- Record keeping systems
- Training
- Fraud
- Internal systems of control
- An evaluation of the accounting system's professional ethics
- An evaluation of sustainability within the accounting system

The next chapters contain more detail on both internal control systems and fraud and after you have studied them you may add to your SWOT analysis. We have also only included three of the above areas in this section of our sample report at the back of this workbook; working methods and practices, record keeping systems and training. We have kept Fraud and Internal Controls, Ethical evaluation and Sustainability evaluation for separate report sections. This breaks up this section and makes it more manageable to write and review.

Once you have completed the SWOT analysis you may then wish to complete a separate PEST analysis. Again, you would put the actual PEST analysis in the appendices and include a summary of the results in the report. In both cases you must make reference to the appendices in the main body of the report.

Whilst carrying out these analyses, it is possible that you have will noticed areas that could present the possibility for a breech of the AAT Code. Note the word **possibility**; it is not necessary for there to have been an actual ethical breech for concern to be raised. The possibility for a breech is sufficient and you should record any such findings for inclusion in your report.

You should also review the systems at this stage specifically for any such possibilities of ethical breeches.

Next, you should carry out a sustainability review of your chosen areas of the system, by considering it against sustainability principles. This will involve considering social, corporate and environmental issues. You should then go on to identify where the organisation can take responsibility for its own actions. For example it could take measures to reduce energy usage, minimise the levels of waste generated in the production of goods or services, or by considering the effects the organisation has on society.

You should at this point have identified detailed weaknesses within the system and be able to write up recommendations to improve the situation. The recommendations may be included in a separate section or sub section of your report entirely. There must be a recommendation for each of the weaknesses you have identified, and they should appear in the same order as the weaknesses. This makes your final report easier to read and more logical. The recommendations should be in sufficient detail so as to clearly explain why they should be implemented, and the benefit to the organisation that would result.

It may be that one recommendation would cover several of the weaknesses, if this is the case the recommendation does not need to be repeated but it should be clear as to which of the weaknesses it covers.

At this point you should not detail the costs and benefits to the organisation of your recommendations, other than brief reasons as to why they should be implemented. The costs and benefits will be included in a later section.

Checklist

- Decide which part of the accounting system you will analyse, ensure you discuss this with your assessor.

- Complete a SWOT analysis on your chosen system or part of a system.

- Put the SWOT analysis in the appendices.

- Write a summary in the main report.

- Refer to the appendices.

- Complete a PEST analysis, if appropriate, on your chosen system or part of a system. Ensure it is in the appendices, with reference to it in the main report.

- Review the accounting systems to ensure there are no actual breaches or possibilities of breaches of the AAT Code.

- Review the accounting systems against sustainability principles.

- Put the ethics and sustainability reviews in the appendices.

- Write a summary in the main report.

- Write a sub-section/main section on recommendations to improve the system, ensuring each weakness you have identified is addressed in turn.

- Ensure all recommendations are fully explained in relation to the benefit they will bring to the organisation.

- Write short, individually numbered paragraphs.

- Write only in the third person.

Case Study Advice

The Case Study contains a lot of information about the whole accounting function in the organisation and you are not expected to write this section of your report on all of it.

Instead, read it through carefully and decide on one section of the system (perhaps payroll or accounts payable (purchase ledger)) to analyse. Ideally you will also investigate this part of the system when looking into internal controls and fraud risk. Perhaps pick the system in respect of which you have the most practical experience or the one that appears to have the most room for improvement.

If in doubt, discuss this with your assessor and remember that if the detail contained within the case scenario is weak then you can supplement it with your own research or knowledge of the work place. Also remember to ensure that the report reads as if you work in the organisation and are making the recommendations to your own manager.

FAQS

1   **I am not sure which part of the accounting system to investigate – which should I choose?** – This depends on your particular organisation and accounting system. The system you choose to investigate should not be so large that it will take you months of research and take pages to document and not so small that it is not sufficient in importance in your organisation. A good guide would be to consider the size of your organisation and the number of staff working on the various systems and processes. Anything that takes up a small amount of one member of staff's time is probably too small. Any system that takes several staff to operate could be too large. If in doubt discuss this with your assessor.

2   **I want to investigate more than one system – is this OK?** – This is dependent on the size of the system(s) and the amount of work involved. Remember that the overall finished report should be approximately 4,000 to 5,000 words (excluding the appendices) and that you do not want to spend too long on this section of your report as you have other key sections to complete. If your organisation has requested that you investigate several areas and this is going to add practical value to your finished report then discuss this with your assessor.

3   **I am investigating the system in this section: how do I keep this separate from my review of internal controls and fraud?** – The analysis of the accounting system section also includes sub-sections on internal controls and fraud. You will see in Chapter 6 that you are required to complete a Fraud Matrix as part of this work, and therefore to specifically address the potential for fraud within the system. As you complete your SWOT analysis though you will automatically consider weaknesses within the controls in place. If the weaknesses relate specifically to internal controls and/or fraud then put them under these headings in your report. If the weaknesses are more general then address them under other appropriate headings. It is more important to ensure the weaknesses are included, and recommendations made to address them, than their precise position in the analysis.

4   **Should I draw a system flow chart?** – A detailed flow chart is required. Your aim is to map the processes and flow of the system so that the reader of your report can gain an understanding of how the system works.

5   **Why should I put the flow chart, SWOT and PEST analysis in the appendices rather than the main report?** – A professional document such as this should not include any tables, charts or diagrams in the main body of the report. These are kept to the appendices to be referred to when required. This will also help to keep your word count down!

6   **I am struggling to think of opportunities and threats in respect of my system, what can I do?** – You could address this section by asking your

supervisor or manager to suggest some. Another idea is to conduct a little research into the overall environment in which the organisation operates. If after these two possibilities you are still finding this difficult then do not worry as including the strengths and weaknesses are far more important.

7   **Any recommendations I come up with are never going to be implemented by my organisation so what should I do?** – This does not matter. The outcome of this unit should be a professional management report making recommendations to improve the organisation. They do not have to be implemented and while it is hoped that they would at least be reviewed and considered by management this does not actually have to happen.

8   **My organisation has really efficient and effective systems in place – so there will be no recommendations to improve** – This is fine as long as you can demonstrate to your assessor that you have fully researched all of the areas of investigation and from that research you have concluded that there are no improvements to be made. It would be rare for a report to contain no recommendations at all.

chapter 5:
INTERNAL CONTROLS

────── **chapter coverage** 📖 ──────

In this chapter we will define internal control, providing examples that relate to both the meeting of organisational requirements and statutory ones. We will provide examples of control activities for three key accounting functions – sales, purchases and payroll.

We will then review the aims and objectives of internal audit within an organisation, or the need for similar activities in an organisation that is perhaps too small to have an internal audit department.

We will look at the assessment of control risk and how it might assess the integrity of any controls in place.

We will then cover how to include internal controls within the analysis of the accounting system section of your report, perhaps adding to the SWOT analysis already prepared as part of Chapter 4.

Finally we will include tips for those writing their report from the AAT Case Study scenario.

INTERNAL CONTROL

Organisations need good, robust internal control systems in order to reduce the risk of fraud and ensure that accounting systems operate appropriately and change as the environment around them changes.

Internal controls are barriers in place within an organisation to protect it from fraudulent activities and human error and to ensure that it complies with applicable laws and regulation. They ensure that the organisation is working to meet its aims and objectives.

An example of an internal control is segregation of duties where the same member of staff does not open the post, record cheques received and also bank them. More examples are provided later in this chapter.

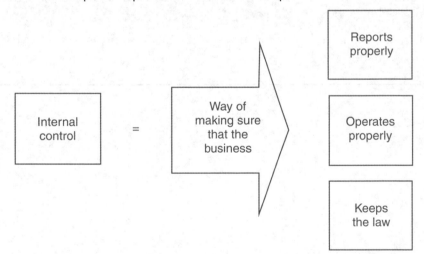

A system of internal control includes procedures and processes designed and implemented to address the risk that the aims and objectives of an organisation will not be met.

A system of internal control consists of the following elements:

- The control environment
- The risk assessment process
- The information system – covered by Chapter 4
- Control activities
- Monitoring of controls

Control environment

The CONTROL ENVIRONMENT is formed by the attitudes, awareness and actions of management and those responsible for ensuring that the internal controls within an organisation meet that organisation's needs.

In other words, the control environment is the foundation on which any internal control system rests. The owners or management of an organisation can introduce numerous controls to ensure that nothing goes wrong, but if everyone ignores them, and management do nothing about that, then the internal control system is not likely to operate very well.

There are various ways that a good control environment can be seen in practice:

- Management communicate and enforce integrity and ethical behaviour
- Management and staff are well trained and competent
- Management operates in a way that promotes control
- The organisation is structured in a way that promotes control
- Authority and responsibility for controls is assigned to people
- Human resources policies promote controls

Size of organisation

The size of an organisation will have an impact on the control environment.

Task 1

In what ways do you think the control environment will be affected by the size of an organisation?

Think about the control environment that might exist in a small organisation such as Cookridge and Cookridge Carpets Limited, in the sample AAT Case Study at the back of this workbook, and in a large multinational organisation. Review the suggested solutions at the back of this workbook once you have attempted this task.

The risk assessment process

As noted above, the internal control system is all about responding to risks that the company's objectives might not be met.

We have already reviewed the AAT's sample Case Study scenario. By way of example, we can look at Cookridge and Cookridge Carpets and conclude that it has the following risks with regard to the three identified business objectives:

1   **Reporting accurately** – The owner and most of the accounts team have no formal accounting qualifications and therefore no knowledge of reporting requirements. Also, record keeping is poor and there is no central accounting system.

2   **Operating effectively** – The accounts team are not all in the office at the same time, most are part time and work different days. The Directors have recently been absent from work without adequate cover. If one of the Directors were to become ill (or if members of the accounts team were to) there is no adequate cover. The business operates with few formal controls and is based on trust in the integrity of staff.

3   **Keeping within applicable laws and regulations** – The business sells some items that are regulated, but the Directors are not legal experts in this area. Also there is no expert in accounting and payroll regulations and no person responsible for ensuring the business remains up to date with regulations and law.

These are not the only business risks Cookridge and Cookridge Carpets face.

All organisations will have some sort of process (not necessarily formal) for assessing the risks it might face and then implementing strategies (controls) to mitigate the risks.

Going back to the risks identified, we can now review the actions the Directors might have taken in respect of the risks.

1   **Reporting properly** – No formal accounting qualifications are held by the Directors or staff – this used to be partly mitigated by the use of a third party to complete the payroll (a highly regulated function), but this is no longer the case. The Directors are keen to support staff who wish to train and obtain qualifications but leaves them to organise this themselves.

2   **Operating properly** – The Directors left signed cheques to be used during their absence, so that suppliers and staff could continue to be paid, and has now employed one full time member of staff in the accounts department.

3   **Keeping the law** – Very little has been done here according to the scenario. It would be expected that the Directors are experienced in some of the regulations affecting the business but this has to be implied, it is not explicit. The scenario does mention that the company has a firm of accountants,

Southampton Accounting Services, and it could be that they provide appropriate advice to it regarding accounting regulations and payroll law.

Size and type of organisation

Clearly the risks facing a business will be different from one organisation to another and will also be affected by whether a company is large or small and whether it operates in a highly regulated industry or not.

In terms of risk assessment, it may be the case that a smaller organisation tends to do this with the assistance of external advisers. For example, a small organisation may be reliant on the business advice that auditors might give in conjunction with their audit, whereas a larger organisation will rely more on internal staff and may even employ people specifically to assess risks to the business.

Task 2

We are now going to look at another organisation, Metal Extrusions Midlands Limited (MEM).

MEM is a family business which is 80 years old. It has 6 family members on the board of directors, four of whom are active in the business. It employs 50 staff; 40 in manufacturing, 10 in administration. The administration department includes a finance department with a staff of five, including a financial controller. The financial controller is a qualified accountant and is not on the board of directors. None of the directors has any accounting skills.

MEM produces metal extrusions, which is a highly mechanised operation. It has always carried out its operations in the same factory. The factory and its machinery are very old. MEM made a significant investment in new machinery in 1954. There have been few developments in metal extrusion since that time. However, the company has been experiencing competition in recent years from a new company set up by two disgruntled former employees.

MEM has several suppliers of metals and the other materials required for production. There are two major suppliers, one of which is British and the other is French. The company purchases 30% of its metal raw materials from the French supplier, which insists on invoicing and being paid in Euros.

What business risks can you identify, particularly with regard to the business objectives of (1) reporting accurately (2) operating effectively and (3) keeping within applicable laws and regulations?

Control activities

CONTROL ACTIVITIES are the policies and procedures that help ensure that management objectives are carried out.

There are a variety of control activities that can be used by an organisation:

- Performance reviews – comparing budgets to actual performance.
- Information processing – checking that transactions have been processed accurately, completely and have been appropriately authorised.
- Physical controls – controls over the physical security of assets.
- Segregation of duties – making sure that a number of people are involved in recording each transaction to minimise opportunity for fraud and error.

The precise control activities used will depend on the business and its risks. However, there are some common control activities that are used in many organisations, and we shall look at these in more detail when we look at sales, purchases and wages.

Control activities may include the following:

Approval and control of documents

Transactions should be approved by an appropriate person, for example, overtime should be approved by departmental heads.

Controls over computerised applications

These may be general controls (see below) or application controls which may be built into the system (see below).

Controls over arithmetical accuracy

For example, when invoices are raised or received, a staff member should ensure that the invoice adds up correctly.

Maintaining control accounts and trial balances

You should know from your accounting studies that these can be useful in ensuring that mistakes have not been made in the financial records. For example, some errors will result in a trial balance not balancing.

Reconciliations

Reconciling two different sources of information, such as a bank statement and a cashbook, or a purchase ledger account and a statement from the supplier can also highlight if errors have occurred.

Comparing assets to records

Again, this can identify where errors have been made in recording transactions. For example, staff might compare non-current assets owned by the organisation to those recorded as owned in the non-current asset register or cash in the petty cash tin to the amount shown in the petty cash book.

Restricting access

A good way of restricting errors and particularly the fraud or theft is to restrict access to assets and financial records – for example, by locking receipts in a safe until they go to the bank, having codes to unlock the cash tills and locking the stores where inventory is kept.

Application computer controls

APPLICATION CONTROLS are controls relating to the transactions and standing data relevant to each computer-based accounting system.

Controls can be found over **input** to the computer (covering completeness, accuracy and authorisation) **processing** and **standing data**.

For completeness, the person inputting the data might check processed output to source documents on a one to one basis, or might check the number of transactions processed with the number of original documents. There might be an agreement of the total value of the amount processed (a batch total) between the source documents and the total input to the computer.

For accuracy, the computer might have programmed controls to check the plausibility of information being put into certain fields. For example, some fields might be wrong if they were a negative number, or the VAT field might have to be a sensible percentage (20% or 5%) of the total field. Invoice numbers might have to have a letter as well as number values to be valid. Scrutinising output will also help to check accuracy.

Checks over authorisation will be manual – checking to see if the source documentation input has been evidenced as authorised by suitable personnel.

Controls over processing will be similar to the above. In addition, there may be a control built into a programme that warns the user if they try to log out before processing is finished.

Controls over standing data will involve regular reviews of the data to ensure that it is correct and controls like hash totals (for example, of number of personnel on the payroll) to ensure no unauthorised amendments have been made.

General computer controls

GENERAL COMPUTER CONTROLS are controls other than application controls relating to the computer environment. They aim to establish a framework of overall control over the computer information system's activities to provide a reasonable level of assurance that the overall objectives of internal controls are achieved.

Controls will exist over developing computer applications, preventing unauthorised changes to applications, testing genuine changes when they are made, and preventing applications being used by the wrong people at the wrong time.

General computer controls include matters of security – limiting access to computers or computer programmes, both physically (by locking them up) and by using passwords, or creating back ups of important files and then keeping them safe – and procedures over development and testing – isolating development and testing, obtaining approval.

Segregation of duties is also an important general control over computers – as other users of the same programmes would notice unauthorised changes to programmes.

Size of an organisation

Control activities are likely to be similar, regardless of the size of the organisation. However, the personnel involved in carrying out control activities may vary. We have already mentioned in the context of the control environment that in smaller organisations, management may be more involved in actually implementing control activities.

Segregation of duties can be a serious problem for small organisations, where often there are insufficient staff to allow proper segregation between duties to occur.

Task 3

Look back to the descriptions of the information systems at Cookridge and Cookridge Carpets Ltd. What do you think of the degree of segregation of duties operating in these systems?

Think about what is appropriate to an organisation such as Cookridge and Cookridge Carpets Ltd which is small and with limited finance staff. Could further segregation be implemented? Think this through carefully and then review the suggested answers at the back of this workbook.

Monitoring of controls

MONITORING OF CONTROLS is necessary to assess the quality of internal control performance over time.

In many entities, this is a function that is performed by the internal audit department. If there is no internal audit department, it would be done as a matter of course by departmental heads – for example, the sales director is likely to become aware of deficiencies of controls in the sales cycle because it means his department does not function as well as it might.

Size of the organisation

The personnel monitoring the controls will differ depending on the size of the organisation. For example, a small organisation is unlikely to have an internal audit department. In addition, monitoring of controls is likely to be less formal in a smaller organisation.

Limitations of internal control systems

However good any single element of an internal control system is, it can never be perfect, due to certain inherent limitations. The key limiting factors are the fact that people make mistakes and may not operate controls properly in error, and also that people can deliberately circumvent control systems if they want to defraud the organisation.

SALES SYSTEMS

We have looked at internal controls at some length. Now we are going to look at the types of controls that will be found in sales systems and the risks that they are designed to address.

Control objectives in the sales system

Task 4

Think for a moment about what the aims of an internal control system over sales might be, and what risks it might be aiming to mitigate. In doing so, you might find it helpful to think through the stages of the sales process – for both credit and cash sales. It might be helpful to think about Cookridge and Cookridge Carpets Ltd, the example Case Study at the back of this workbook. How does their current sales system operate and what risks are there? When you have thought it through, read through the next section, which gives you some examples of controls.

Here we are focusing mainly on the risk of credit sales. When an organisation is making cash sales, no credit is granted, and often there is no formal order as the customer chooses and pays for goods which are available. Risks associated with cash sales are more in respect of the cash element which is discussed at the end.

Orders and extending credit

- An organisation should only supply goods to customers who are likely to pay for them (**risk** – the organisation loses goods of value and does not receive value in return). This is often termed as only selling to customers with a good credit rating.

- An organisation should encourage customers to pay promptly (**risk** – the organisation loses the value of being able to use the money in their business or interest on the money in the bank due to late payment).

- An organisation should record orders correctly (**risk** – the organisation sends the wrong goods to the customer causing added cost or risk of loss of the customer).

- An organisation should fulfil orders promptly (**risk** – the organisation loses custom).

Despatching and invoicing goods

- An organisation should record all goods it sends out (**risk** – goods are sent out and not invoiced, and the organisation loses money).

- An organisation should correctly invoice all goods and services sold (**risk** – insufficient is charged and the organisation loses money).

- An organisation should only invoice goods it has sent out (**risk** – organisation charges for goods in error and loses custom).

- An organisation should only issue credit notes for a valid reason (**risk** – organisation issues credit notes incorrectly and loses money).

Recording and accounting for sales, credit control

- An organisation should record all invoiced sales in its accounting records (sales ledger and general ledger) (**risks** – sales are not recorded and wrongly omitted from financial statements, and payment is not chased as sale was never recorded).

- An organisation should record all credit notes in its accounting records (**risks** – as above, financial statements likely to be misstated and potential to lose custom by chasing cancelled debts).

- An organisation should record all invoiced sales in the correct sales ledger accounts (**risks** – losing custom by chasing the wrong customer for the debt and not receiving the money from the correct customer).

- An organisation must ensure that invoices are recorded in the sales ledger in the correct time period (**risk** – errors in the financial statements due to counting both the sale and the related inventory (stock) as assets or counting neither).

- An organisation must identify debts for which payment might be doubtful (**risk** – organisation fails to take action until it is too late to retrieve the debt and, in the worst case, organisation wrongly records bad debts as assets in the financial statements).

Receiving payment (cash)

- An organisation should record all money received (**risk** – the money could be stolen or lost, custom could be lost through chasing payments already made by the customer, the financial statements are likely to be misstated).

- An organisation should bank all money received (**risk** – the money could be stolen or lost (with consequences as above), the organisation loses out on interest that could be being made on receipts).

- An organisation should safeguard money received in the period until it is banked (**risk** – money may be stolen in the interim period).

Task 5

For each of the objectives given in bullet points above, can you think of a procedure (a control) which will help achieve the objective? When you have thought it through, read through the next section, which gives you some examples of controls.

Controls in the sales system

We shall list some examples of controls in the sales system relating to the objectives outlined above, but before we do, it is relevant to emphasise the importance of segregation of duties in a sales system.

Task 6

Which stages of the sales system do you feel ought to be dealt with by different staff members, and why? Read through the following text to see the answer.

It is possible that a person could create a false customer in order to steal the organisation's inventory (stock) and then not pay for it. This would only be possible if the same person were in charge of orders and credit control/accounts receivable (sales ledgers).

There are two key potential frauds with regard to the receipt of cheques and/or cash from customers. First, a staff member may intercept cheques when they arrive at the organisation and steal them before they are recorded. Second, a staff member may steal cheques and/or cash and misallocate them to the accounts receivable (sales ledger) records (in other words, make it look as if the customer is further behind in payment than he actually is on an ongoing basis). Such a fraud may not be discovered as the customer may never appear behind enough in payments to be chased for overdue debts.

In order to prevent such frauds, several people should be involved in dealing with cheque and/or cash receipts.

Orders and extending credit

- Credit terms offered to customers should be authorised by senior personnel and reviewed regularly.

- Credit checks should be carried out on new customers.

- Changes in customer data (for example, their address) should be authorised by senior personnel.

- Orders should only be accepted from customers with no existing payment problems.

- Order documents should be sequentially numbered so that 'false sales' can be traced.

Despatching and invoicing goods

- Despatch of goods should be authorised by appropriate personnel and checked to order documents.

- Despatched goods should be checked for quality and quantity.

- Goods sent out should be recorded.

- Records of goods sent out should be agreed to customer orders, despatch notes and invoices.

- Despatch notes should be sequentially numbered and the sequence should be checked regularly.

- Returned goods should be checked for quality.

- Returned goods should be recorded on goods returned notes.

- Customers should sign despatch notes as proof of receipt.

- Invoices should be prepared using authorised prices and quantities should be checked to despatch notes.

- Invoices should be checked to ensure they add up correctly.

- Credit notes should be authorised by appropriate personnel.

- Invoices and credit notes should be pre-numbered and the sequence should be checked regularly.

- Inventory records should be updated from goods sent out records.

- Sales invoices should be matched with signed delivery notes and sales orders.

- Orders not yet processed should be regularly reviewed.

Recording and accounting for sales, credit control

- Sales invoice sequence should be recorded and spoilt invoices recorded and destroyed.
- Sales receipts should be matched with invoices.
- Customer remittance advices should be retained.
- Sales returns and price adjustments should be recorded separately from the original sale.
- Procedures should exist to record sales in the correct period.
- Receivables statements should be prepared regularly.
- Receivables statements should be checked regularly.
- Receivables statements should be safeguarded so they cannot be amended before they are sent out.
- Overdue accounts should be reviewed and followed up.
- Write off of bad debts should be authorised by appropriate personnel.
- The accounts receivable control account should be reconciled regularly.

Receiving payment (cash)

- There should be safeguards to protect post received to avoid interception.
- Two people should be present at post opening, a list of receipts should be made and post should be stamped with the date opened.
- There should be restrictions on who is allowed to accept cash (cashiers or sales people).
- Cash received should be evidenced (till rolls, receipts).
- Cash registers should be regularly emptied.
- Tills rolls should be reconciled to cash collections which should then be agreed to cash banked.
- Cash shortages should be investigated.
- Cash records should be maintained promptly.
- There should be appropriate arrangements made when cashiers are on holiday.
- Receipts books should be serially numbered and kept locked up.
- Cash and cheques should be banked daily.
- Paying in books should be compared to initial cash records.
- All receipts should be banked together.
- Opening of new bank accounts should be restricted to certain personnel and authorised by senior management.
- Cash floats held should be limited.

- There should be restrictions on making payments from cash received and restricted access to cash on the premises.

- Cash floats should be checked by an independent person sometimes on a surprise basis.

- Cash should be locked up outside normal business hours.

Task 7

What are the objectives of the following controls?

- Credit checks should be run on new customers.
- Sales invoices should be sequentially numbered.
- Receivable statements should be prepared regularly.
- Restrictions on who is allowed to receive cash.

You should also run through the lists of controls given in the text above to ensure you can identify the objectives behind each of them.

Task 8

Here is some information relating to sales at XYZ Limited:

Peter receives sales orders in a variety of ways: by telephone, by email and in person. Whenever he receives an order, he notes it in the sales order book. Some orders can be fulfilled from shop inventory (stock), others must be ordered from suppliers.

When an order is delivered, Peter raises a despatch note on his computer. The computer automatically raises an invoice when a despatch note is raised. These documents are printed off and sent to the customer. When the documents are printed, the computer programme automatically updates the sales daybook which is also on the computer.

When customers pay, Peter enters the details of the cheques into the cashbook.

Some of the controls in the system have been highlighted. Some of these are manual controls and others are computerised. For instance, orders are manually recorded in the order book, but sales invoices are automatically listed in the sales daybook as a result of a computer programme.

The system at XYZ Limited is very basic and is far from perfect. Can you recommend any other controls that should exist in the system as outlined above?

List out as many as you can, that are appropriate to XYZ Limited, before reviewing the suggested answers at the back of this workbook.

PURCHASES SYSTEMS

Control objectives in the purchases system

Task 9

Think for a moment about what the aims of an internal control system over purchases might be, and what risks it might be aiming to mitigate. In doing so, you might find it helpful to think through the stages of the purchases process. When you have thought it through, read through the suggestions set out below.

Ordering

- An organisation should only order goods and services that are authorised by appropriate personnel and are for the organisation's benefit (**risk** – the organisation pays for unnecessary or personal goods).

- An organisation should only order from authorised suppliers (**risk** – other suppliers may not supply quality goods or may be too expensive).

Receipt of goods and invoices

- An organisation should ensure that goods and services received are used for the organisation's purposes (**risk** – the organisation may pay for goods/services for personal use).

- An organisation should only accept goods that have been ordered (and appropriately authorised) (**risk** – as above).

- An organisation should record all goods and services received (**risk** – the organisation fails to pay for goods/services and loses suppliers).

- An organisation should ensure it claims all credits due to it (**risk** – organisation pays for goods it does not use.

- An organisation should not acknowledge liability for goods it has not received (**risk** – organisation pays for goods it has not received).

Accounting

- An organisation should only make authorised payments for goods that have been received (**risk** – as above).

- An organisation should record expenditure correctly in the accounting records (**risks** – financial statements are misstated, and the organisation does not pay for genuine liabilities).

- An organisation should record credit notes received correctly in the accounting records (**risks** – financial statements are misstated, and the organisation pays for items unnecessarily).

- An organisation should record liabilities in the correct accounts payable (purchase ledger accounts) (**risk** – organisation pays the wrong supplier).

- An organisation should record liabilities in the correct period (**risk** – financial statements are misstated by recording purchase but not inventory or recording inventory, but not the associated liability).

Payments

- An organisation should only make payments to the correct recipients and for the correct amounts which are authorised (risk – organisation pays the wrong supplier).

- An organisation should only pay for liabilities once (risk – the organisation pays more than once and the supplier does not correct the mistake).

Task 10

For each of the objectives given in bullet points above, can you think of a procedure (a control) which will help achieve the objective? When you have thought it through, read through the next section, which gives you some examples of controls.

Controls in the purchases system

We shall list some examples of controls in the purchases system relating to the objectives outlined above, but before we do, it is relevant to emphasise the importance of segregation of duties in a purchases system.

Task 11

Which stages of the purchases system do you feel ought to be dealt with by different staff members, and why? Read through the following text to see the answer.

The key areas of concern are:

A person could order and pay for personal goods through the organisation, so ordering and payment should be separated. The risk of fraud will also be reduced if the person who writes out the cheques is different from the person who signs the cheques.

BPP
LEARNING MEDIA

Ordering

- An organisation should have a central policy for choosing suppliers.

- The necessity for orders should be evidenced before orders are authorised.

- Orders should only be prepared when purchase requisitions are received from departments.

- Orders should be authorised.

- Orders should be pre-numbered and blank order forms should be safeguarded.

- Orders not yet received should be reviewed.

- Supplier terms should be monitored and advantage should be taken of discounts offered.

Goods and invoices received

- Goods received should be examined for quality and quantity.

- Goods received should be recorded on pre-numbered goods received notes.

- Goods received notes should be compared with purchase orders.

- Supplier invoices should be checked to orders and goods received notes.

- Supplier invoices should be referenced (numerical order and supplier reference).

- Supplier invoices should be checked for prices, quantities and calculations.

- Goods returned should be recorded on pre-numbered goods returned notes.

- There should be procedures for obtaining credit notes from suppliers.

Accounting

- Purchases and purchase returns should be promptly recorded in daybooks and ledgers.

- The accounts payable (purchase ledger) should be regularly maintained.

- Supplier statements should be compared with accounts payable.

- Payments should be authorised and only made if goods have been received.

- The accounts payable (purchase ledger) control account should be reconciled to the list of balances.

- Goods received but not yet invoiced at the year end should be accrued separately.

Payments

- Cheques should be requisitioned and requests evidenced with supporting documentation.

- Cheque payments should be authorised by someone other than a signatory.

- There should be limits on the payment amount individual staff members can sign for.

- Blank cheques should never be signed.

- Signed cheques should be despatched promptly.

- Payments should be recorded promptly in the cashbook and ledger.

- Cash payments should be limited and authorised.

Task 12

What are the objectives of the following controls?

- The necessity for orders should be evidenced.
- Supplier invoices should be matched to goods received.
- Supplier statements should be compared with accounts payable.
- Blank cheques should never be signed.

You should also review the list of all the controls given above and ensure that you understand what the objectives of the controls are.

WAGES SYSTEMS

Control objectives in the wages system

Task 13

Think for a moment about what the aims of an internal control system over wages and salaries might be, and what risks it might be aiming to mitigate. In doing so, you might find it helpful to think through the stages of paying wages and salaries. When you have thought it through, read through the next section, which gives you some examples of controls.

BPP
LEARNING MEDIA

Setting wages and salaries

- An organisation should only pay employees for work they have done (**risk** – the organisation overpays).

- An organisation should pay employees the correct gross pay, which has previously been authorised (**risk** – the organisation overpays).

Recording wages and salaries

- An organisation should record gross pay, net pay, and relevant deductions correctly in the payroll records (**risk** – organisation may make incorrect payments to staff/tax offices and financial statements may be misstated).

- An organisation should record payments made in the bank and cash records and general ledger (**risk** – financial statements may be misstated).

Paying wages and salaries

- An organisation should pay the correct employees (**risk** – angry, unpaid workforce and/or the organisation pays the wrong people).

Deductions

- An organisation should ensure all deductions have been properly calculated and authorised (**risk** – breaking the law, incorrect pension contributions).

- An organisation should ensure they pay the correct amounts to taxation authorities (**risk** – breaking the law and incurring fines).

Task 14

For each of the objectives given in bullet points above, can you think of a procedure (a control) which will help achieve the objective? When you have thought it through, read through the next section, which gives you some examples of controls.

Controls in the wages system

We shall list some examples of controls in the wages system relating to the objectives outlined above, but before we do, it is relevant to emphasise the importance of segregation of duties in a purchases system.

Task 15

Which stages of the wages system do you feel ought to be dealt with by different staff members, and why? Read through the following text to see the answer.

Where there is no segregation of duties it would be possible for the person responsible for the wages system to authorise an inappropriate salary for himself, or enter someone who is not an employee onto the payroll.

Setting wages and salaries

- Personnel records should be maintained and referred to when calculating wages and salaries.

- Engaging employees, setting rates of pay, changing rates of pay, overtime, non-statutory deductions from pay and advances of pay should all be authorised and recorded.

- Changes in personnel should be recorded.

- Hours worked should be recorded, time should be clocked.

- Hours worked should be reviewed.

- Wages should be reviewed against budget.

Recording wages and salaries

- Payroll should be prepared, checked and approved before payments.

Paying wages and salaries

- Wage cheque for cash payments should be authorised.
- Cash should be kept securely.
- Identity of staff should be verified before payment.
- Distributions of cash wages should be recorded.
- Bank transfer lists should be prepared and authorised.
- Bank transfer lists should be compared to the payroll.

Deductions from pay

- Separate employees' records should be maintained.

- Total pay and deductions should be reconciled month on month.

- Costs of pay should be compared to budgets.

- Gross pay and total tax deducted should be checked to returns to the tax authorities.

Task 16

What are the objectives of the following controls?

- Changes in personnel should be recorded.
- The wage cheque for cash payments should be authorised.
- Costs of pay should be compared to budgets.

You should also review the list of all the controls given above and ensure that you understand what the objectives of the controls are.

INTERNAL AUDIT

Internal audit is a function within an organisation that is independent from the managers. This independence is vital as one of the duties of the internal audit function is to review and test internal controls that management have implemented, and to make recommendations to improve them.

The internal audit department will usually report to an audit committee, which for large organisations will include non-executive directors of the organisation.

Many smaller organisations will not have an internal audit department and may outsource the internal audit function to third parties such as their external auditors.

Internal auditors are primarily concerned with improving internal controls. They do this by performing internal audits of various functions within the organisation. They will look at whether the policies and processes in place are designed and operating effectively and make recommendations to improve them.

Internal auditors are also an important tool in risk management in an organisation. They will monitor and evaluate the organisation's risk management processes, and whether these processes protect the owners of the organisation in terms of their investment within it. For example they will review how the accounting systems of the organisation are kept secure, free from error and backed up in case of a system crash.

Internal auditors will also use risk assessment to review which areas of the organisation are at the greatest risk of a loss of controls and prioritise their activities accordingly. A typical internal audit project will include the following processes:

1   Decide and communicate the scope and objectives of the audit.

2   Review and map the relevant area of the organisation. This could include interviews with staff as well as documenting systems and processes with tools such as flowcharts.

3   Ascertain the key risks in the area under review.

4   Identify the current controls in place.

5   Test that the controls are effective, by identifying a sample of the controls to test, and then adjusting the sample based on the results of the testing.

6   Document the work done and report to management with recommendations to improve.

7   Follow up to ensure that the recommendations have been implemented appropriately.

REPORT

When completing this section of your report you will need to complete a review of the internal control systems in place within the area of the accounting system that you have chosen to evaluate. This could include reviewing recent internal audit reports if appropriate.

This may have already been part completed as part of your system SWOT analysis (covered in Chapter 4). Remember that controls include system controls, manual controls, personnel controls and accounting controls.

Start a new section in your report entitled **Internal Controls and an Analysis of Fraud** and write a summary of the current controls in place. Depending on the size of your organisation there may have been visits by the internal audit department. If this is the case then include the results of recent visits in your review (and put a copy of relevant reports, if your manager approves this, in your appendices).

From this review of controls you should highlight weaknesses in the current controls, and be able to include recommendations to improve them in your recommendations sub section. Remember that all weaknesses identified must be addressed by recommendations.

Checklist

- Complete a review of the current controls in place within the organisation and or the chosen system.

- Include a review of recent internal audit reports if appropriate.

- Start a new section of your report entitled Internal Controls and an Analysis of Fraud.

- Write a summary under a sub heading Internal systems of control.

- Include any documents reviewed in the appendices if possible.

- Make recommendations to improve the current controls, where appropriate.

- Write short, individually numbered paragraphs.

- Write only in the third person.

Case Study Advice

Within the case study you will need to review the internal controls in place within the organisation and also the accounting system, or part of the accounting system you have chosen to investigate.

If the specific information contained within the scenario is lacking in detail then supplement it with your own research or knowledge of the work place (for example, you may need to research good controls that should be in place within a purchase ledger system) and discuss this with your assessor if unsure.

In the sample answer in the back of this workbook the student has included a range of issues relating to the internal controls at Cookridge and Cookridge Carpets, from across the accounting system. Depending on the scenario you are using you may wish to focus on one section of the accounting system in particular.

One way to review the controls in place is to review the critical incidents that have occurred. For example inventory levels are recorded on Excel spreadsheets and the warehouse manager should update the spreadsheets when inventory is delivered into the warehouse, or when inventory is moved from the warehouse into the showroom. However, when the new warehouse manager, Joe Bloggins, was appointed he carried out an inventory check and found that there was a shortfall of £3,000 in the actual physical inventory against that on record. This was because there was no evidence of when goods had been taken from the warehouse to the showroom. This shows that the internal control in place – the spreadsheets that should be updated every time inventory levels change or items of inventory are moved – was not working effectively.

FAQS

1   **My organisation has good controls, how can I complete this section?** –
    Within this section you are investigating the controls in place and analysing
    them to determine whether they are adequate or not. From this you can
    conclude as to whether there are recommendations to make to improve the
    controls. If you conclude that there are no recommendations to be made
    because good controls exist then this is acceptable, but unlikely!

2   **How can I research possible controls that should be in my chosen
    system?** – One way of doing this is to work backwards, start at the current
    controls in place and then investigate what they could possibly be in place to
    prevent. You could also search the Internet for examples of your chosen
    system and controls ie you could search for 'examples of purchase ledger
    controls'. You could also look at critical incidents that have occurred that
    have highlighted a lack of controls, or that controls are not being
    implemented.

3   **My organisation does not have an internal audit department – How do I
    cover this in my report?** – You do not need to worry if your organisation
    does not have an internal audit department. In the sample case study, there
    is no such department due to the size and the ownership of the organisation.
    This section's focus is on internal controls, and this can still be covered.

4   **My organisation has an internal control department but they will not
    allow me to review its recent reports – is this a problem?** – No, you can
    still complete your own review of the internal controls in place in your
    chosen part of the accounting system and make recommendations to
    improve them.

5   **Any recommendations I come up with are never going to be
    implemented by my organisation so what should I do?** – This does not
    matter. The outcome of the ISYS paper should be a professional
    management report making recommendations to improve the organisation.
    They do not have to be implemented and while it is hoped that they would
    at least be reviewed and considered by management this does not actually
    have to happen.

chapter 6:
ANALYSIS OF FRAUD

LEARNING OUTCOMES
2.3 – Explain methods that can be used to detect fraud within an accounting system
2.4 – Explain the types of controls that can be put in place to ensure compliance with statutory or organisational requirements
2.5 – Explain how an internal control system can support the accounting function
3.4 – Identify potential areas of fraud arising from a lack of control within the accounting system evaluating the risk
6.2 – Identify the effects that any recommended changes would have on the users of the system
6.3 – Enable individuals to understand how to use the accounting system by use of: ■ Training ■ Manuals ■ Written information ■ Help menus

WHAT IS FRAUD?

Fraud is deception of some sort which in the situation of a commercial organisation will involve either:

- Misappropriation of assets
- Misstatement of the financial statements

Misappropriation of assets

In its simplest form, this is the theft of assets such as cash or inventory. However there is a variety of different and subtle ways in which this can be accomplished:

- Theft of cash
- Theft of inventory
- Teeming and lading
- Fictitious employees
- Fictitious suppliers
- Fictitious customers
- Collusion with customers
- Collusion with suppliers
- Receipt of invoices for bogus supply of goods or services
- Disposal of assets

Misstatement of the financial statements

In this type of fraud the financial statements are deliberately manipulated in order to falsify the position of the company. This could be by over-stating assets or profits or by under-stating the results and the profits.

Examples of this type of fraud are:

- Over-valuation of inventory
- Not writing off irrecoverable (bad) debts
- Manipulation of depreciation charges
- Fictitious sales
- Understating expenses

These lists are not exhaustive, you should try to think of any possibilities of fraud within your chosen system.

Task 1

Reading through the sample Case Study at the back of this work book consider all the probable frauds that could occur within the accounts department of Cookridge and Cookridge Carpets Ltd – even if the controls currently in place make such a fraud unlikely. List as many as you can.

FRAUD CONTROLS

There are many different controls that can be used within organisations to prevent fraud. One key point to note however is that the controls in place must be appropriate to the organisation, taking into account such factors as its ownership, size, staffing etc.

Fraud controls can be grouped into the following categories:

Staff controls – such as supervision, segregation of duties, good recruiting processes (including the following up of references), training and membership of professional bodies.

Management controls – such as effective, well trained managers, authorisation of journals, control limits on expenditure and purchases and authorisation levels for activities. This would also include an internal control or audit role.

Physical controls – such as keeping asset registers or assets under lock and key, access controls to offices and other places of work. Also controlling access to systems as discussed in Chapter 4.

General controls – such as double checking calculations, reporting on exceptions, signing for wages received and rules and procedures in place for staff.

The fraud matrix

A FRAUD MATRIX is a useful tool to assist organisations with investigating the potential for fraud within a system, and analysing the controls currently in place to prevent them. The matrix then grades the potential for fraud, according to risk. Although this is subjective, it enables a risk based approach to improving controls that are appropriate to the organisation under investigation.

The risk to the organisation is graded perhaps 1 = low and 5 = high and then possible improvements to the controls for all high and or medium activities can be recommended.

A simple matrix is set out below.

Potential fraud	Controls currently in place	Risk to the organisation	Implications	Improvement identified
1				
2				
3				
4				
5				

To assist you with adequately investigating the fraud controls in place within your chosen organisation you will be expected to complete a fraud matrix, preferably on the part of your system that you have chosen to investigate within Chapter 4. The matrix would be placed in the appendices to your report and the body of the report would include a section summarising your findings, with reference to the appendix, and make recommendations to improve the current controls.

To ensure you cover this section to the required sufficiency you should ensure that you include at least five potential frauds in your research.

Task 2

Potential fraud	Controls currently in place	Risk to the organisation	Implications	Improvement identified
1				
2				
3				
4				
5				

Taking 5 of the potential frauds analysed in Task 1 construct a fraud matrix, to detail the current controls in place, the implications of fraud to the organisation, the risk to Cookridge and Cookridge Carpets Limited and recommendations to improve the controls. Ensure the recommendations you make are appropriate to the organisation.

EXAMPLES OF FRAUD

In this section we will review specific examples of fraud that might take place within certain accounting systems, namely:

- Accounts receivable (sales ledger) fraud
- Accounts payable (purchase ledger) fraud
- Payroll fraud

We will also consider examples of the types of controls an organisation might put in place to prevent them.

Examples of accounts receivable fraud

Fraud within the accounts receivable (sales ledger) system is possible because the system involves the receipt of money, especially where this is in the form of cash, from customers for goods or services sold to them. Examples of such frauds might be:

- Stolen cash receipts – cash received is not recorded in the ledgers and is instead taken by employees.

- Overcharging on sales – goods sold are overcharged, with employees keeping the additional amount received from customers.

- Inflating customer orders – with additional goods being retained by employees for own use or to sell on privately.

- Writing off debts – writing off amounts owed and then possibly also keeping any payments made.

- Raising credit notes to reduce amounts owed and then keeping part of any payment made.

- Teaming and lading – allocating one customer's payment to another in order to balance the books and detract from a shortfall.

One of the controls in place to prevent such examples of fraud might be good company records of goods sold with reconciliations to actual inventory in place.

Task 3

Considering each of the potential accounts receivable frauds identified above suggest a suitable control that might reduce the risk of fraud for a medium sized organisation.

What other, more general, examples of controls can you suggest to reduce the risk of accounts receivable fraud?

Examples of accounts payable fraud

Fraud within the accounts payable (purchase ledger) system is possible because the system includes the ability to order goods from suppliers and then to make payments. Possible examples include:

- Ordering goods for own use – and then paying for them through the organisation's accounts payable.

- Fictitious suppliers – making payments to suppliers that do not exist using personal bank accounts to receive the money.

- Paying for genuine goods, but instead of paying suppliers paying the money into personal bank accounts.

- Teeming and Lading – paying into private bank accounts payments owed to suppliers, and then using later payments to pay to the original suppliers and so on, constantly using funds allocated to alternative suppliers to pay off the earlier debts, with the hope that this will hide that an amount of money owed has not been paid.

One of the controls in place to prevent such examples of fraud would be segregation of duties with organisations not allowing the same member of staff to place orders with suppliers, book in goods received and then process payments to them.

Task 4

Considering each of the potential accounts payable frauds identified above suggest a suitable control that might reduce the risk of fraud for a medium sized organisation.

What other, more general, examples of controls can you suggest to reduce the risk of accounts payable fraud?

Examples of payroll fraud

There is a risk of fraud within the payroll system because the system involves the payment of money that could be misappropriated. Examples of such fraud might be:

- Ghost employees – having more employees on the payroll than physically exist within the organisation.

- Overstating overtime pay – paying for more hours than physically worked.

- Increasing hourly rate/salary – paying a higher hourly rate or salary than contracted for.

- False expense reimbursement claims – expenses are often paid through payroll and false claims may be processed this way.

- Keeping employees on the payroll once they have resigned – and amending the bank details so that the pay is paid into own/third parties account.

- Unofficially recruiting new staff – and adding their details to the payroll system.

One of the controls in place to prevent such a fraud would be the competence and integrity of the person completing the payroll. This might be strengthened if that person has a payroll or accounting qualification, and is a member of a professional body such as the AAT. There are other, more specific, controls that can be put in place to lower the risk of payroll fraud.

Task 5

Considering each of the potential payroll frauds identified above, suggest a suitable control that might reduce the risk of fraud for a medium sized organisation with 2 payroll staff.

What other, more general, examples of controls can you suggest to reduce the risk of payroll fraud?

THE IMPACT OF FRAUD ON THE ORGANISATION

Fraud impacts an organisation in a variety of ways:

Financial – fraud involves the theft of funds or assets from an organisation. This in turn affects its profitability and the owner's investment in the organisation. It can also impact a company's share price.

Reputation – exposure of fraud can affect an organisation's reputation with all internal and external stakeholders. This in turn could lead to loss of business.

Employee morale – the trust of existing employees could be damaged. Future recruitment and retention of staff might also be affected.

Depending on the organisation type the owner(s) of the organisation that will suffer as a result of fraud will be different, and may take different actions on discovery of fraud taking place.

In the UK the Serious Fraud Office (SFO) offer advice and guidance to organisations on dealing with suspected fraud and offer a service for organisations and employees to report serious or complex fraudulent activities.

www.sfo.gov.uk

Less serious fraud can be reported to Action Fraud www.actionfraud.org.uk

REPORT

When completing this section of your report you will need to complete an analysis of the risk of fraud within your organisation or part of the system chosen. This will include completing a fraud matrix.

This may have already been part completed as part of your system SWOT analysis (covered in Chapter 4).

In the section of your report entitled Internal Controls and Analysis of Fraud write a summary of the analysis of fraud and risks, under a sub heading – **Analysis of Fraud**. Make reference to your fraud matrix, constructed from your analysis of possible frauds, in your appendices.

From this analysis of the risk of fraud you should highlight weaknesses (sometimes referred to as deficiencies) in the current controls, and be able to include recommendations to improve them. Remember that all weaknesses identified must be addressed by recommendations.

Checklist

- Complete a Fraud Matrix on your chosen system or part of a system.

- Grade the risk to the organisation of each fraud occurring.

- Put the Matrix in the appendices.

- Write a summary in the main report.

- Refer to the appendices.

- Make recommendations to improve the current controls, where appropriate.

- Write short, individually numbered paragraphs.

- Write only in the third person.

Case Study Advice

As with the accounting system section you should pick one area of the Case Study scenario to cover for this section.

If the specific information contained within the scenario is weak then supplement it with your own research or knowledge of the work place (for example, you may need to research the types of fraud that might occur within a purchase ledger system) and discuss this with your assessor if unsure.

FAQS

1   **My company has good controls and fraud is unlikely, how can I complete this section?** – Within this section you are investigating all the possible frauds that could occur and analysing the current controls to determine whether they are adequate or not. From this you can conclude as to whether there are recommendations to make to improve the controls. If you conclude that there are no recommendations, because good controls exist, then this is acceptable.

2   **Can the fraud risk matrix be included in the body of the report?** – You should keep all tables, charts and diagrams in the appendices to a professional report and make reference to them in the body of the report.

3   **How can I grade the risk of the fraud occurring?** – To do this construct your own, simple, grading system. Perhaps a grade of 1 = low risk of occurring and 5 = high risk of occurring.

4   **How can I research possible frauds in my chosen system?** – One way of doing this is to work backwards, start at the controls in place and then investigate what they could possibly be in place to prevent. You could also research the Internet using a search engine and searching for examples of your chosen system fraud ie you could search for 'examples of accounts payable or purchase ledger fraud'.

5   **Any recommendations I come up with are never going to be implemented by my organisation so what should I do?** – This does not matter. The outcome of the ISYS paper should be a professional management report making recommendations to improve the organisation. The recommendations do not have to be implemented and while it is hoped that they would at least be reviewed and considered by management this does not actually have to happen.

chapter 7:
COST BENEFIT ANALYSIS AND COMPLETING YOUR REPORT

chapter coverage 📖

This chapter looks at the requirement that the recommendations made in the report be fully supported by a cost benefit analysis. Such an analysis is an important part of any report that makes recommendations. It helps any decision maker reading the report to understand the costs associated with the implementation of the recommendations and the benefits that will be gained from doing so.

As part of this report you will be expected to explain all or some of your recommendations in terms of the costs and benefits of implementation. How many you justify will depend on how many recommendations you have made. You will be expected to explain and quantify the costs and benefits where possible between those that are tangible, and can be quantified, and those that are intangible – these are hard to quantify in monetary terms. You should also consider the opportunity costs of any actions and this chapter will help you understand how to consider these.

Finally you need to consider the impact of your recommendations, in terms of costs and benefits, on the organisation and its staff, including their training needs and response to change.

LEARNING OUTCOMES
3.1 – Identify an organisation's accounting system requirements including hardware and software packages
3.5 – Review methods of operating for cost effectiveness, reliability and speed
6.1 – Make recommendations for changes to the accounting system including ethical and sustainability considerations, with a clear rationale and an explanation of any assumption made
6.2 – Identify the effects that any recommended changes would have on the users of the system
6.3 – Enable individuals who operate accounting systems to understand how to use the accounting system by use of training, manuals, written information and help menus
6.4 – Identify the implications of recommended changes in terms of time, financial costs, benefits and operating procedures

COST BENEFIT ANALYSIS

The Cost Benefit Analysis (CBA) takes your recommendations and analyses them in terms of the costs and benefits to the organisation of implementing them.

Both costs and benefits can be categorised under the headings of tangible and intangible.

Tangible – these are costs and benefits that are easy to value in terms of time and/or money.

For example, if recommending a new computer system then tangible costs would include:

- The cost of the system itself
- The loss of staff time while they are training
- The cost of future licences and improved speed of processing

Wherever possible in your CBA you should include tangible costs with an estimate of them.

You would not be expected to get detailed quotations or information to support your recommendations but you should make estimates as to what the costs will be as this will aid the reader of your report in making any decisions as to whether to implement the recommendations.

Task 1

A firm of accountants has decided to train all new staff in basic bookkeeping as part of their induction programme. What tangible costs might there be to such a decision?

What would your estimates of these costs be? Think of costs not just in terms of money spent but also in relation to time and any other quantifiable measure.

Intangible – these are costs and benefits that cannot be quantified in financial terms. (Not to be confused with **intangible assets**, which can be and are quantified.)

For example a new computer system may: Improve the motivation and morale of staff.

Although happier, more motivated staff may be more efficient resulting in an increase in organisational productivity, this is more difficult to value in monetary terms.

Task 2

What would be the intangible costs of the training outlined in Task 1? Try to jot down as many as you can and then review our suggested answers at the back of this workbook.

For the recommendations you make in your report there should be some intangible costs and/or benefits identified.

These do not have to have estimated values assigned to them but as they are often powerful persuaders for implementing a recommendation they should be included so that the decision maker can consider all the issues fully.

Task 3

What tangible and intangible benefits might there be to such training as part of an induction programme for new staff?

Try to think about why an organisation would want to include this training as part of such an programme. When you have listed both tangible and intangible benefits then review the suggested answers at the back of this workbook.

Opportunity cost – another important type of cost to include is the opportunity cost of the recommendation. An opportunity cost can be defined as the value of an activity which has not taken place, because of a decision to do something else.

For example, in the tasks above, the organisation has chosen to send all new staff on a bookkeeping course. When completing the tasks you will (hopefully) have listed both tangible and intangible costs and benefits of this decision. One of the costs we have included in our example answers is an opportunity cost. Can you see which one?

The answer is that the revenue lost, because the new staff are not working for clients and therefore are not generating chargeable hours, is an opportunity cost of the decision. Where possible try to identify the opportunity costs of your recommendations.

REPORT

The Cost Benefit Analysis can either go in your report as a new chapter, before the appendices, or as an appendix in itself.

Which approach you choose may be influenced by the overall word count of the report so far, remember that this does **not** include the appendices.

Whichever approach you choose, ensure your Cost Benefit Analysis is referred to in your executive summary as it is an important part of the overall report (see below).

To complete your Cost Benefit Analysis ensure that you consider at least two or three of your main recommendations and cover both the tangible and intangible costs and benefits of them. Where possible, you should also try to identify opportunity costs and include estimated values for all of your tangible costs and benefits.

Case Study Advice

Within the case study you may not have access to detailed financial information such as staff wages and salaries. In order to complete your CBA you will have to estimate the tangible costs and benefits of the recommendations you have made.

If estimates of costs and benefits are difficult to express in terms of monetary value then ensure you quantify them in other ways such as time.

COMPLETING YOUR REPORT

If you have been following this workbook as you complete your actual report then you should now have completed much of the work required.

BPP
LEARNING MEDIA

This chapter covers the other sections of your report which are necessary in order to pull it together into a completed final report ready for assessment by your assessor.

The sections of the full report are:

- Title Page
- Contents Page
- Terms of Reference
- Executive Summary
- Methodology
- Introduction to the Organisation
- The Accounts Department
- Review of the Accounting System
- Ethical Evaluation of the Accounting System
- Sustainability Review of the Accounting System
- Internal Control and Analysis of Fraud
- Recommendations to Improve
- Cost Benefit Analysis
- Appendices

As you will now have completed the main areas of your report and made some recommendations to improve the organisation's accounting systems and internal controls, we will now look at each of the remaining sections in turn.

Apart from the first two, the title page and the contents page, each must be included as numbered sections to your report with the individual paragraphs numbered as per the guidance in the rest of this workbook.

Title page

The title page of your report should contain a meaningful title, your full name and your AAT student registration number.

A meaningful title might be:

A report analysing the Internal Controls in place and Evaluating the 'Accounting System' of XYZ PLC.

Your title should reflect both the name of your organisation and the system you have chosen to investigate.

The title page should also contain an authenticity statement. This is where you confirm that the work undertaken to complete the report is your own, and unaided and that it is a true reflection of the organisation.

Warning – Completing, by signing and dating, this statement means that you are testifying that the work is your own and unaided. Your report should not include any material copied from sample reports such as the one at the back of this workbook, or from other students' work. Submitting work which is not your own may result in your assessor reporting you to the AAT's conduct and compliance team.

Contents page

This should set out the page and section number of each part of your report. It is also recommended that you include a word count on this page of the total number of words in your report, excluding the appendices.

Most word processing packages include a word count facility. To check the word count in Microsoft Word click on Tools, Word Count and the total number of words will be calculated. Remember not to include your appendices in the word count.

An example contents page would look like this:

Contents		
Section:		**Page:**
1	Terms of Reference	2
2	Executive Summary	3
3	Methodology	4
4	Introduction to the Organisation	5
5	The Accounts Department	6
6	Review of the Accounting System	7
7	Ethical Evaluation of the Accounting System	9
8	Sustainability Review of the Accounting System	11
9	Internal Control and an Analysis of Fraud	12
10	Recommendations to Improve	13
11	Cost Benefit Analysis	14
	Appendices	16
Word Count: 4,056 words		

Terms of reference

This should be a short section that explains to the reader exactly what the report sets out to do. It explains why it is being written and the areas it covers.

The terms of reference for the ISYS report can also include that you are completing the report as part of your AAT Level 4 Diploma in Accounting studies. This would not be included in a professional business report but is relevant to why you have produced this work and can be included here.

As with the whole report, none of this section should be written in the first person, ie you should not use the words 'I' or 'my'.

Methodology

This will show how you planned and investigated your report ie questionnaires, books, internet etc.

Executive summary

This is a short, summarised version of the overall report that sets out the main findings for the reader.

Imagine that you have commissioned a report into a possible re-structuring of your company and have recruited some consultants to do this for you – they have produced for you a 10,000 word report detailing their findings, recommendations and rationale behind them.

Although you would probably want to read through the full report at some stage you would also want a summarised version to set the overall scene before you do so, detailing the main recommendations and a brief explanation of why they have been identified.

This is what an executive summary does.

The AAT guidance on the executive summary states that it should be:

'A short (two or three paragraphs only) overview of the report's findings and the benefits that the organisation will gain by following the recommendations within the report'

Therefore in your report it should be no more than 2 to 3 paragraphs long and should summarise your main recommendations and reasons for them.

This does, briefly, repeat the recommendations which you will also include in your main report but this is important to set the scene for your reader before they become involved with the detail.

Your executive summary must also refer to your Cost Benefit Analysis as this is an important part of summarising the overall costs and benefits of the recommendations made.

Other sections

You should now include the other sections of your report as laid out in this text:

- Introduction to the Organisation
- The Accounts Department
- Review of the Accounting System
- Ethical Evaluation of the Accounting System
- Sustainability of the Accounting System
- Internal Control and Analysis of Fraud
- Recommendations to Improve

- Cost Benefit Analysis
- Appendices

Ensure that all pages and paragraphs are numbered and that the appendices are also numbered, and referred to in the main report.

The **Appendices** can be split down further to include:

Appendices to the report – eg organisation charts, SWOT analysis, Fraud Matrix etc.

Mapping to the standards – Your report is required to be fully mapped to the standards and therefore to the assessment criteria and learning outcomes. In order to do this you require a mapping sheet that sets out all the standards for this paper. Next to each criterion list the paragraph numbers that demonstrate that you have shown competence in it. An example mapping is included in the sample report at the back of this workbook.

As you map your work you may find that some of the more technical learning outcomes are not covered fully by your report, for example you may have referred to income statements but not explained their use in decision making.

The AAT have allowed this report to have technical notes in the appendices, if required, to strengthen areas such as this. For advice on how to complete the technical notes see below.

Once your mapping is complete you must then review whether all the standards have been covered by your report. If not then you may need to add to it in order to strengthen it. If you are unsure about this then you should discuss this with your assessor.

Technical Notes – If an assessment criterion is not covered in the report (or not to the depth required by the assessor), then this can be covered within a written explanation included in the appendix.

This allows you to cover some of the more technical learning outcomes of the standards as part of technical notes in the appendix. An example of this is in appendix 4 of the sample report at the back of this workbook.

Please note that this should only be completed by exception, and that the main report should map to, and demonstrate competence in, as many of the standards as possible.

If you are unsure about how to complete the technical notes then you should discuss this with your assessor.

Manager's authenticity statement – where the report has been based on your workplace, the final appendix to include is a manager's authenticity statement. This will confirm that the work is your own and unaided and that the report is a true reflection of the organisation. This must be signed and dated, include your manager's full contact details, and must also be printed on your organisation's headed paper.

ANSWERS TO CHAPTER TASKS

CHAPTER 1   **The basic principles of ISYS**

No tasks

CHAPTER 2   **Introduction to the organisation**

1   The aims and objectives common to most types of organisation:

-   Provide goods and/or services
-   Employ staff
-   Manage cash flow
-   Control internal systems effectively
-   Keep expenditure and/or revenue within budgets
-   Manage stakeholder expectations
-   Efficiency
-   Customer satisfaction
-   Public reputation

Differences in aims and objectives – public and private sector organisations:

-   Public sector – social/ethical issues, provision of service, equality of access to service

-   Private sector – sales, profit, share price, survival

Organisation type affects the organisation's approach to all the factors identified above.

2   Other factors that affect an organisation might include:

-   Customers
-   Suppliers
-   Employees
-   Culture
-   The environment within which it operates
-   Owners
-   Age
-   Size
-   Strategy

- Market
- Wealth
- Status
- Structure
- Product or service offered
- Skills of the workforce

3   The advantages of a tall organisation structure include:

- Narrow span of control – easier for management to manage a few employees

- Clear management structure

- Clear lines of responsibilities

- Clear lines of control

- Employees can see a clear progression ladder, which can feel more achievable

- Structure suited for larger organisations

The advantages of a flat organisation structure include:

- More freedom and responsibility for employees

- Quicker decision making that is not hindered by many levels of management

- Quicker communication from top to bottom

- Less management cost

- Improved team working

- Less bureaucracy

4   Internal stakeholders include:

- Employees
- Management
- Owners

External stakeholders might include:

- Community groups
- Customers
- Suppliers
- The Government
- Regulatory bodies
- Society
- Payables (creditors)
- Shareholders

- Schools, colleges & universities
- Competitors
- Professional associations
- Industry trade groups
- Landlords

Information needs of internal stakeholders might include all financial and management reports (see Chapter 4) plus other ad-hoc and regular reports that meet the stakeholders' needs.

External stakeholders may wish to have some of the information that internal stakeholders have access to but it would not always be in the organisation's best interest to provide it! Organisations can have different approaches to different external stakeholders – often dependent on their individual power and influence over the organisation. Some information may also need to be provided to meet regulatory requirements – eg Tax returns.

Organisations meet both the information needs of internal and external stakeholders through effective Management Information Systems (MISs) and this will include accounting systems.

CHAPTER 3   The accounts department

1   Advantages of a centralised accounts department include:

- Greater senior management control of the department's activities
- Standard, consistent procedures
- Decisions can be made taking into account the 'big picture' or the organisation as a whole
- The organisation can employ, and benefit from the skills and experience of, more senior, qualified managers and accountants
- In uncertain times the organisation will benefit from strong, central leadership
- Reporting may be quicker and benefit from standard report layouts and central information

The disadvantages of a centralised accounts department might include:

- Less decision making, and therefore empowerment of junior staff
- Accountants and managers at a central location may lose touch with the operational side of the organisation, weakening decision making abilities
- Senior management can be tied up making decisions that should be made lower down the organisation

- Communication and interaction between the accounts department and other functions of the organisation my be impaired

- Other parts of the organisation might resent controls being imposed by a central accounting department due to a lack of knowledge and appreciation of the department's requirements

2   To demonstrate what reports could be prepared we have used the sample Case Study scenario at the back of this work book. At present there seems to be very few, if any, management accounting reports prepared. Those that would benefit the organisation might include:

- A budget
- Variance report – budget to actual sales
- Variance report – budget to actual costs
- Inventory report – values of inventory
- Inventory report – age of inventory
- Profitability reports – different product lines
- Aged debt report
- Overhead costs – apportioned to products sold
- Cash flow forecasts and statements
- Wages and salaries – average employee wage, overtime worked etc

Such reports would provide the Directors with a snapshot of the business and the key financial data that affects its profitability. For each of the above reports you should be able to review the value it would add to decision making regarding the organisation. The more information management and Directors have, the better informed decisions they can make.

3   There are both internal and external stakeholders to the accounts department of Cookridge and Cookridge Carpets Limited:

Stakeholder		Information needs
Internal	Owners – John and Peter Cookridge	The Directors require accurate financial and management reporting information. They require a complete set of financial reports including the statement of profit and loss and the statement of financial position plus management reports as listed as part of the answer to task 2 above. This will enable them to make much better informed decisions regarding the business. It is clear from the scenario that the organisation's cash flow has not been proactively managed and, at least once, the owners have had to contact the bank to request temporary increases to their overdraft limit in order to allow them to pay a customer. An emergency banking of cash from the tills has also occurred in order for a direct debit to be honoured. This is a good example where better information would have led to improved decision making.
	Showroom staff	They require accurate completion of their wages and salaries. The warehouse supervisors would also benefit from reports such as aged inventory reports to enable them to better manage the warehouse inventory.
	Accounts staff	Each of the accounts staff performs a separate, distinct role with regard to the preparation of the accounts and each is an internal stakeholder to the department as a whole. Each requires data and information plus good communications with each other.

Stakeholder		Information needs
External	HM Revenue & Customs	The accounts department are responsible for preparing the information that will lead to the calculation of the tax due to HM Revenue & Customs. This will include national insurance contributions, corporation tax, VAT and PAYE tax and so it will require timely, accurate information in order that the correct tax is paid. However, although the accounts department is responsible for this, the scenario also shows the power the owners have in this case. The accounts clerk was instructed to record expenses relating to the office Christmas party in a manner that she knew breached the current HMRC rules, yet still went ahead and did it for fear of repercussions from the owners.
	Customers	The accounts department in Cookridge and Cookridge Carpets Limited is responsible, through the accounts receivable clerk, for granting credit to new and existing customers. The customers will want information on the credit limit granted to them and also statements regarding how much they owe.
	Suppliers	Suppliers to Cookridge and Cookridge Carpets Limited are stakeholders to the accounts team through the accounts payable clerk. Suppliers want to be paid accurately, and on time.
	Bank manager	The bank of Cookridge and Cookridge Carpets Limited has had to contact the company in the past to warn them that the overdraft limit has been reached. The company frequently reach this limit as a result of poor cashflow. The bank is a payable (creditor) of the business and will perhaps ask to see accurate cash flow forecasts to enable them to see that the overdraft can be reduced within the time scales set.

There are many information needs not currently being met in Cookridge and Cookridge Carpets Limited as there is very little financial and management reporting taking place. The above examples set out the information needs of key stakeholders. They also demonstrate where better information could have led to more informed decision making. The Directors of the organisation, and perhaps the new Senior Accounts Clerk, requires a full,

BPP
LEARNING MEDIA

accurate and timely set of financial and management reports. At present this is not being completed due to a variety of reasons, including the lack of a centralised accounting system.

CHAPTER 4   Accounting systems

1   Advantages of a centralised system might include:

- All data is stored in one central place so greater control
- Improved security
- Staff can all use the same system leading to efficiencies in training etc
- Centralised reporting
- Consistent reporting
- Quicker access to information

Advantages of a decentralised system might include:

- Each individual system can be more relevant to that area of the organisations needs

- Lower risk of errors/breakdowns affecting the whole organisation

- Lower level staff might have more control and autonomy over their system thus improving morale

- Quicker access to information from each, individual system

Cookridge and Cookridge Carpets Limited is better suited to a centralised system so that all staff can be trained to use one system and can then cover each other's roles or access information if required. It will also enable financial reports to be quickly and easily provided to the owner for management decision making.

2   The advantages of having a user manual for all of the activities that take place within an accounts department include:

- Quick and efficient training of new staff
- Better visibility of the controls in place
- Consistent approach to completing activities
- Easier to rotate staff between roles and responsibilities
- Easier to evaluate staff
- Improved supervisory and management control
- More effective time management

Disadvantages of such an approach might be:

- Increased risk of 'outsiders' being able to operate the system

- Procedures may stifle innovation and improvements to processes

- User manuals take time to complete

- The manuals may become out of date quickly

- The manuals need to be tested to ensure they accurately reflect the systems in place

- Staff often do not conform to manuals, negating the benefits of having them

3   An organisation might put in place the following rules regarding the use and control of passwords.

- Passwords must not be written down

- Passwords must not be shared

- Passwords must be changed regularly

- Passwords must not be generic

- When staff leave, access must be cancelled on the day they leave the department

- Access can only be set up for new staff with management authorisation

- Staff access to different parts of the system must be regularly reviewed

It is important that these types of rules and controls are in place to protect the integrity of the system and the organisation. If one password is used by all staff (generic) then there is little point in using them as the whole system is open to all. This lack of control then increases the risk of errors, from staff using parts of the system they are not trained to, and fraud.

It is also important that new access to the system is controlled so that staff are not granted access to parts of the system they do not require and that as staff leave, their access is cancelled promptly so that they can not continue to use the system, and other staff can not use their passwords. Often organisations make sharing of passwords a disciplinary offence to ensure that controls are maintained.

4 A system flowchart for the accounts payable function might be:

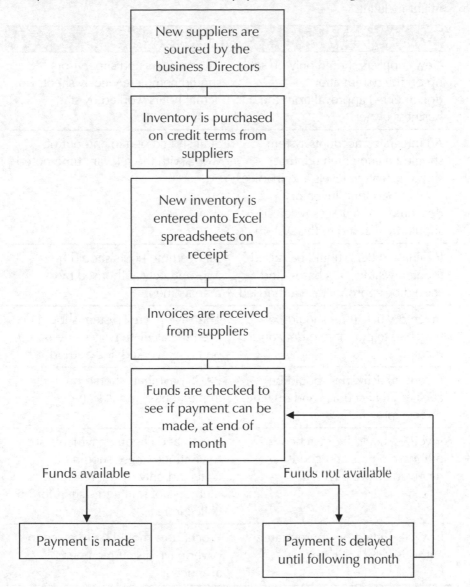

Recommendations to improve the accounts payable and payroll systems might include:

Accounts payables system:	Payroll system:
New suppliers should only be set up on the system after documented approval from the business owner	All managers and supervisors should complete weekly sheets on actual hours worked by staff
An integrated accounts system should be implemented, that shows inventory levels and invoices due for payment. Inventory delivered and invoices received should be entered to this system	Staff should sign in and out of work, with the relevant time noted
Purchase orders should be raised for all inventory purchases, and should be appropriately authorised	All overtime hours should be appropriately authorised by management
Inventory deliveries should be matched to purchase orders on receipt	The Sage payroll system should be used to calculate wages due based on hours worked and authorised
Inventory deliveries should be checked for accuracy and quality on receipt	BACS payments should be implemented for all staff
Invoices should be matched to purchase orders and goods received before payment	If cash and cheque payments are to continue, these should be collected only by the relevant members of staff and signed for on collection
Invoices should be appropriately authorised for payment	Procedures should be in place to cover payroll staff member's absence
Payments to suppliers should follow standard payment terms	

Note: The above improvements are in relation to the interpretation of the accounting system in the scenario. The scenario is not explicit about the type of controls in place regarding some of the activities taking place. It has therefore been assumed they are not in place and have included them in the improvements (and in a report they would be reflected in the recommendations made). It may be assumed that all or some are in place, just not detailed specifically in the scenario. Either approach is fine.

5   An example SWOT analysis for Cookridge and Cookridge Carpets Limited might include:

Strengths	Weaknesses
■ An open plan accounts office ensures that when staff are in and working with each other they can communicate freely and cover each others work when absent. ■ The cheque book is kept in a locked desk in the office – but see weaknesses. ■ Current inventory system has good detail included. ■ Credit reference agency used to decide whether to grant credit. ■ Credit control procedures in place. ■ Controls re: cash and cheques coming into the office – manual day book then accounts. ■ Staff seem keen to improve systems – Accounts receivable clerk has implemented some initiatives.	■ As most accounts staff are part time there are often occasions when no one is in the office. Because all staff can access the office and the accounts system with common passwords there is a risk of lack of control. There will also be issues concerning communication between staff as they are not all in the office at the same time. ■ Poor access control to the accounts office. Keypad entry system is not used and door is propped open. Can be accessed via the same stairs that are used by customers of the showroom. ■ Stand alone computers with no central system means that the system does not produce central, standard reports for key stakeholders. ■ Staff, as a whole, are not qualified in accounting which poses a risk of errors and relaxed controls and also a lack of accountability. ■ There appears to be a lack of planning in the work of the accounting team, highlighted by the fact that when the payroll was first bought in house a temping agency was contracted to run it for the first two months. This could have led to errors and inconsistencies in the work, and therefore within the hand over of the system to the payroll clerk once employed. ■ Showroom and warehouse staff are paid in cash which poses a risk of theft.

Strengths	Weaknesses
	▪ Office staff are paid by cheque – there is a risk of cheques being stolen and fraudulently used.
	▪ Manual calculation of weekly payroll is a weakness as it can lead to errors or fraudulent increases in staff pay.
	▪ Cash is withdrawn to pay wages – as above, any use of cash.
	▪ Debts are often not followed up further to the initial phone call.
	▪ On at least one occasion the cheque book was accessed by other members of staff as the drawer it is kept in was found to be unlocked.
	▪ Staff are not trained in excel and could make errors.
	▪ No further check on new credit customers other than credit reference agency.
	▪ It is possible to set up new credit customers in the system without having gone through the required credit reference checks.
	▪ Lack of controls over new starters in the payroll and HR system. New starters can be set up with very little information and no documentary evidence or approval.
	▪ Manual completion of invoices, on Word, could lead to errors.
	▪ Cash is not counted when removed from the tills on weekdays.
	▪ Poor controls surrounding petty cash, leading to frequent discrepancies of amount and IOUs.
	▪ Inappropriate use of petty cash as a pay day loan.

Strengths	Weaknesses
	■ No contingency planning – staff able to take on each others roles when absent.
	■ No controls or authorisation over changes to contracted agreements with existing suppliers.
	■ Staff can not use each others systems.
	■ No control on authorisation – signing of blank cheques to cover absence.
	■ No controls on payments to customers.
	■ Lack of controls on staff hours have led to incorrect rotas and staff pay.
	■ Two weeks pay packets completed in advance – this is a weakness as too much cash was in the office.
	■ Wages should be completed correctly, not in advance and adjusted later.

Opportunities	Threats
■ There is an opportunity to use one central accounts system on networked computers which will ensure that there is better cover for work when staff are absent and better reporting of key financial data to relevant stakeholders.	■ Having the accounts prepared on Excel poses a risk that errors can be made to the spreadsheets that will not be easily identified, and therefore the inventory and accounting information may be incorrect.
■ There is an opportunity to train staff in accounting and also in the systems they use, making them much more aware of the controls and procedures they should be operating with and also more efficient.	■ There is a threat to the physical security of both the accounts office and the staff employed in that department due to the lack of entry controls to the office.
■ There is an opportunity to train staff in each others roles – perhaps	■ There is a threat to the office and its systems by the common use of one

Opportunities	Threats
with a back-up member of staff for each. This could motivate staff and also ensure cover during absence.	password across the organisation – any staff who wanted to could access the office and the accounting systems.
	■ The lack of formal procedures and control in respect of accounts payable and receivable has led to an overdraft that the bank has asked to be repaid. This is a cash flow threat to the organisation.
	■ There appears to be no back-up taken of the current systems which is a threat as if the systems in use failed key financial data would be lost.
	■ Regulatory environment – this is constantly changing, for example potential changes to VAT rates. The accounting system needs to recognise these changes and react accordingly.
	■ While a relationship with a debt collection agency is in place, this is rarely used due to the costs involved. This may mean that debts are never recovered.

6   The correct answer is:

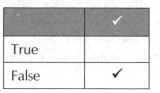

	✓
True	
False	✓

Straightforwardness and honesty are related to the fundamental principle of integrity.

7   The correct answer is:

	✓
If they are asked for during legal proceedings	✓
When your manager tells you to disclose the information	
When writing a report for general circulation within your organisation	

In this case you have a legal duty to disclose the information.

8   An example ethical review for Cookridge and Cookridge Carpets Limited might include:

CURRENT PRACTICE	PRINCIPLE BREACHED AND DETAILS	RECOMMENDED PRACTICE
Disclosure of personal details (address and telephone number) of a member of staff to an individual on the telephone.	CONFIDENTIALITY There is a requirement to, in accordance with the law, respect the confidentiality of information acquired as a result of professional and business relationships and not disclose such information to third parties without proper and specific authority unless there is a legal or professional right or duty to disclose.	▪ Personal details of staff should be stored in accordance with the Data Protection Act and not disclosed without the permission of the employee in question, or unless there is a legal or professional right or duty to disclose.
Christmas party bill was split in order to get around HMRC tax deductable expense limits.	PROFESSIONAL BEHAVIOUR By asking Margaret to breach HMRC rules in relation to the bill for the Christmas party, John has failed to comply with relevant laws and regulations. By failing to confront John rather than carrying out his request, Margaret has assisted John in breaching this principle.	▪ The full £160 does not qualify as a tax deductable expense and as such should not be treated as one. ▪ HMRC rules should be fully complied with at all times.

CURRENT PRACTICE	PRINCIPLE BREACHED AND DETAILS	RECOMMENDED PRACTICE
John asked Paula to produce a set of accounts that show the company in the 'best possible light' in order to secure a bank loan.	**INTEGRITY** Producing accounts designed to mislead the bank as to the position of the company represents a lack of honesty. To comply with the fundamental principle of integrity, a member must be straightforward and honest in all professional and business relationships.	• Accounts should be prepared that show the company in a true and fair light.
Peter placed an exceptionally large order with a supplier on the basis that the supplier had promised to sponsor his next motorcycle show if the order was increased. Peter has a favourite group of suppliers he likes to use, mainly because they are sometimes willing to sponsor his motorbike and racing efforts.	**OBJECTIVITY** A member shall not allow bias, conflict of interest or undue influence of others to override professional or business relationships. Peter is allowing conflict of interest to affect his professional relationship and judgment. He should be selecting suppliers based on the value for money they can offer, not those that offer personal favours in exchange for the business.	• A formal approved supplier list should be established. • Where an approved supplier is not in place, a minimum of three quotes should be obtained and the supplier that offers the best value for money should be chosen.

9 Your answer will depend on the nature of your job and the type of organisation that you work for. Good answers would include issues relating to economic factors, social factors and the environment.

CHAPTER 5 Internal controls

1 A larger organisation might have a set of internal controls, whereas it is unlikely that a smaller organisation will. In a small organisation, senior managers may work closely with operational staff and their attitude to controls will be particularly influential.

2 **Business risks at MEM**

(1) Reporting accurately

The fact that the qualified accountant is not on the board may impair the effectiveness of the board to report properly.

The fact that the company deals in more than one currency increases the risk of errors in the financial statements.

(2) Operating effectively

The business is at risk of not operating properly due to out of date machinery.

In addition, the company is facing increased competition from a company which is likely to have more up to date equipment and may have a useful knowledge of MEM's operating practices.

(3) Keeping within applicable laws and regulations

The company has a number of employees and must ensure that it satisfies the many legal requirements in relation to its employees.

The company operates from an old building using old machines. It must ensure that it operates within the boundaries of health and safety law as well.

3 There is very little segregation of duties at Cookridge and Cookridge Carpets Limited and, although the key sales, wages and purchase functions are carried out by different staff, the system would benefit from some segregation being introduced. For example, payments for purchases should be authorised by someone other than Margaret. It would be appropriate for the new, full time, senior accounts clerk (you!) to authorise all such payments.

4 The answer follows the question in the chapter text below it.

5 Examples of controls are given in the next section of the chapter.

6 The answer follows the question in the chapter text below it.

7 Credit checks on new customers are to ensure that the customer is a good credit risk and able to pay for goods/services purchased.

Sales invoices should be sequentially numbered to ensure that fictitious sales invoices are not raised (and used to then misappropriate genuine payments for other invoices).

Receivable statements should be prepared regularly to check that the sales ledger has been kept correctly (customers are likely to draw attention to debts that are not genuine) and to encourage trade receivables (debtors) to pay promptly.

There should be restrictions on who is allowed to receive cash for the business to minimise the risk of cash being stolen or lost.

8 ▪ Sales orders should be recorded on pre-numbered documents.

▪ Despatch notes should be checked to sales orders prior to despatch.

▪ The accounts receivable ledger should be written up more frequently to aid credit control.

▪ Accounts receivable ledger should be reviewed frequently to check for irrecoverable (bad) debts.

▪ Someone other than Peter should record and bank receipts.

9 The answer follows the question in the chapter text below it.

10 Examples of controls are given in the next section of the chapter.

11 The answer follows the question in the chapter text below it.

12 The necessity of orders should be evidenced so that goods are only purchased for genuine business reasons.

Supplier invoices should be referenced so that they can be recorded in sequence and so that they can be found easily in the event of disputes.

Supplier statements should be compared to the accounts payable ledger to discover errors in recording in the accounts payable ledger and/or to discover whether the company is being charged for genuine liabilities.

Blank cheques should never be signed as this makes it easier for cash to be stolen from the company/spent on goods which are not for business use.

13 The answer follows the question in the chapter text below it.

14 Examples of controls are given in the next section of the chapter.

15 The answer follows the question in the chapter text below it.

16 Changes in personnel should be recorded so that the right employees are paid for work done.

A payroll should be prepared to ensure that employees are paid the correct amounts and the correct deductions are made, and posting to the general ledger can be checked.

A wage cheque for cash payments should be authorised so that cash is not stolen.

Costs of pay should be compared to budgets because any discrepancies observed might reveal errors in calculation or in payments made to staff or leavers inappropriately.

CHAPTER 6   Analysis of fraud

1   Frauds that could occur within the accounts department include:

- Theft of assets – computers or other assets could be stolen by any of the staff within Cookridge and Cookridge Carpets Limited due to the easy access to the accounts office.

- Overstatement of wages – there are no controls in place to approve actual wages paid to staff, so the wages clerk could overstate wages by either overpaying on hours worked and/or the hourly rate.

- Theft of cash from the office – petty cash is kept in the staff room and there is little control over access to the office. There is no one member of staff responsible for the petty cash tin and the only control is a sheet on which any expenses paid for using petty cash should be logged. However, this control is currently ineffective as it would appear that it is not being used. Staff also have been borrowing money from this tin on occasions. There are frequently discrepancies over the amount that should be in the tin and surprise at finding the tin empty or running low.

- Theft of cheques – there are few controls in place to store the cheque book securely and it has been found in an unlocked drawer together with blank, signed cheques.

- Overstatement of hours worked – the stores supervisor could add more hours to the staff rotas than physically worked by staff.

- Theft of inventory – there is no mention of controls such as inventory counts to prevent the theft of inventory from the warehouse. The excel spreadsheet used to record movements of, or changes to the level of, inventory is also an ineffective control as staff fail to update it.

- Overpayment of supplier invoices – there is no control to check that cheques prepared to pay suppliers equate to the amount physically owed and invoiced.

- Under recording of goods sold – there are few controls in place to ensure goods purchased are accurately recorded.

- Writing off of debts – there are no controls to ensure that debts from customers are not written off.

- Theft of cash or cheques from the mail – no separate controls are in place to record cash and/or cheques received.

- Theft of cash and/or cheques from tills – the tills are not balanced each evening so there is no accountability for any missing cash and/ or cheques.

- Theft of cash via the set up of a ghost employee – there are no controls over the addition of new starters to the Payroll system, such as a requirement for documentation that cannot be over-ridden, segregation of duties, or linking to HR records. This means that a person could set up a fictional employee and keep the wages 'earned' for themselves.

2 Below we have completed a fraud matrix with suggested improvements to the controls currently in place. It should be noted that there are many possible ways of rectifying identified weaknesses and the ones included within your final report should be relevant to your organisation. For example we could not suggest full segregation of duties within Cookridge and Cookridge Carpets Limited as there are not enough staff working within the accounts department to make this possible! Also the assessment of risk is purely subjective, based on our knowledge of the organisation and the controls currently in place.

It should also be noted that not all these recommendations may be implemented by the management of the organisation, this possibility should not stop you from making the recommendation in your report.

Potential fraud	Controls currently in place	Risk to the organisation 1 = low, 5 = high	Implications	Improvement identified
1. Theft of assets	Physical access to the accounts department controlled by keypad but with common entry code	2	Loss of assets such as computers and possibly key data and information	Access code changed and only key staff have knowledge of it, non-current asset register kept
2. Overstatement of wages – wages clerk	None	4	Overpayment of wages to staff	All wages are countersigned on completion and system used to calculate wages based on hourly rates signed off by management

Potential fraud	Controls currently in place	Risk to the organisation 1 = low, 5 = high	Implications	Improvement identified
3. Theft of cash from the office	Petty cash is kept in the staff room and office has keypad access. Contains notebook for recording expenses charged to petty cash, but this control is often not followed	2	Loss of cash	Door to office should remain locked rather than propped open. Petty cash tin should be stored in locked cupboard or safe. One member of staff should be responsible for the petty cash
4. Theft of cheques	Cheque book kept in locked drawer – but control not always followed	4	Cheques could be used for own purchase/ cash	Cheque book is kept in safe and log of cheques kept to ensure all accounted for
5. Overstatement of hours worked – showroom supervisor	None	3	Overpayment of wages to showroom staff	Staff should sign in and out of work and this should be used for wages calculations and countersigned by showroom supervisor – a more comprehensive control, though perhaps not appropriate to Cookridge and Cookridge Carpets Ltd would be a time keeping system based on staff clocking in and out of work

Potential fraud	Controls currently in place	Risk to the organisation 1 = low, 5 = high	Implications	Improvement identified
6. Theft of inventory from warehouse	An Excel spreadsheet showing inventory levels and location of inventory is in place, however, this document is not always updated and inventory checks back to it do not tend to occur.	4	Loss of inventory	Regular inventory checks and perhaps random checks on staff as they leave work
7. Overpayment of supplier invoices	None	3	Increased costs	Accounting system should be used that matches invoices to purchase orders and goods received, this will produce reports on total payments for reconciliation. Also BACS payments for suppliers
8. Under recording of goods sold	None	3	Reduced revenue	Accounting system linked to tills could be initiated plus supervisory checks on tills. Also inventory checks to identify 'lost' inventory
9. Writing off customer debts	None	3	Increased costs	All debts written off must be authorised by business owner
10. Theft of cash/ cheques from the mail	Cash and cheques received are written into day book	2	Lost cash/ cheques, reduced revenue	Mail opening should be witnessed by an additional staff member

Potential fraud	Controls currently in place	Risk to the organisation 1 = low, 5 = high	Implications	Improvement identified
				Cash and cheques received are double checked by the witness
11. Theft of cash/ cheques from the tills	None – tills are not reconciled until the following day	3	Lost cash/ cheques	Staff are paid an additional 30 minutes at the end of the day and reconcile their own tills before leaving work
12. Theft of wages arising from the payment to a ghost employee	Documentary evidence should be provided before any new starter can be set up on the Payroll system, however, there is evidence that this is not always the case	3	Lost cash/ increased costs	Set up a control in the Payroll system to prevent the set up of a new employee until documentary evidence has been logged. Set up a process of checking and authorisation so that a new starter can only be paid once the new starter and the supporting evidence have been checked and authorised by the senior accounts clerk. This should be done via a separate log in to the Payroll system. Carry our regular checks of the Payroll records against the HR system and vice versa

3 Stolen cash receipts – clear procedures, and segregation of duties, controls for accepting cash payments and recording through the ledgers, also good controls for storage of cash and banking.

Overcharging on sales – sales systems such as bar coding that ensure prices are generated automatically. Authorisation of amendments to prices on system.

Inflating customer orders – segregation of duties and supervisory controls regarding matching orders to goods sent/handed to the customer.

Writing off debts – all debts require management authorisation to be written off.

Credit notes – all credit notes also require management authorisation before they can be processed on the system.

General controls include:

- Reconciliations of key customer accounts
- Spot checks of invoices to customer discounts
- Authorisation of all customer orders over a certain amount
- Not allowing customers to deal with only one member of staff

4 Ordering goods for own use – segregation of duties between ordering, booking goods into inventory and payments, plus supervision of each activity including appropriate authorisations.

Fictitious suppliers – management authorisation of all new suppliers added to the system and reconciliation of payments to invoices, also segregation of duties.

Paying amounts into own bank account – authorisation of all amendments to banking details on the system, segregation of duties between amending details and processing payments.

Teeming and Lading – cash reconciliations, reconciling payments made to suppliers and invoices, segregation of duties.

General controls include:

- Authorisation of all purchase orders

- Ordering from approved suppliers only

- Matching of goods received to purchase orders

- Matching of invoices to purchase orders and goods received

- Payments through BACS only and system generated to reflect invoices processed

5   Ghost employees – reconciling the number of staff on the payroll to physical staff in the organisation plus good controls in connection with adding and removing staff from the payroll system.

Overstating overtime pay – clearly documented overtime rates for staff and management/supervisor authorisation of overtime hours worked.

Increasing hourly rate/salary – clearly documented pay rates plus all amendments to the hourly rate on the system should be countersigned by management. Perhaps also segregation of duties so only one of the payroll staff can amend rates, and the other reviews and gets authorisation for this from management.

False expense claims – all receipts included and travel checked for mileage and to diary. All claims authorised by management.

Keeping employees on the payroll – All resignations have to be officially documented and one member of the payroll staff is responsible for removing them from the system, the other checks this and management countersign.

Unofficial recruitment of new staff – All recruitments have to be officially documented and one member of the payroll staff is responsible for adding staff to the system, the other checks this and management countersign.

Examples of general controls include:

- Exceptions reporting – where the accounting system produces reports that highlight exceptions to the normal payroll such as particularly high payments, hours worked etc. These are checked and countersigned by management

- Management countersigning the payroll staff's own pay

- Spot checks on members of staff's pay to ensure it is accurate in relation to their pay scale and normal hours worked

- No cash payments to staff

- Management checks on the payroll reports to look for duplicate bank details for example

- Rotation of payroll staff

CHAPTER 7 **Cost benefit analysis and completing your report**

1   Tangible costs associated with training might include:

- Cost of training course – say £500 per employee

- Cost of lost chargeable hours (as the staff will not be working on clients accounts) – 5 days × 7.5 hours per day = 37.5 hours at a chargeable rate of, say, £25 per hour = £937.5

- Travel expenses to the training provider – say £15 per day × 5 days = £75

2   Intangible costs might include:

- Other staff discontent as new staff are provided with training they did not have

- Loss of efficiency as new staff's induction is extended and therefore they are not available to work on clients

- Client dissatisfaction due to delays in completion of work due to staff not being available

3   Tangible benefits might include:

- Staff are better trained, so chargeable fee could be increased – from £25 to £30 per hour

- Fewer errors in work completed leading to less supervisor time spent on new staff's work and a reduction in having to amend work completed incorrectly – say 4 hours per week

Intangible benefits might include:

- Staff are better trained in basic knowledge so more motivated and efficient

- Staff morale improves as they feel valued due to the investment in training them

- Clients always see well trained and knowledgeable staff so organisation reputation is enhanced

SAMPLE CASE STUDY AND REPORT

APPROACH TO PRODUCING THIS REPORT

The report that has been produced is a student's first submission onto SecureAssess and is based on an overall review of some of the issues raised. It is not specific to one Accounting System and as such there are many other issues that have not been identified and included within this report. The student's assessor would load feedback onto SecureAssess to help the student understand how the report could be improved.

As this example report is based around a Case Study it is essential to read the whole case study through before deciding how to complete the report. Information that will be required for different sections of the report will be included throughout the case study.

A proposal for the report should then be produced and discussed with an assessor to ensure that the overall approach is correct and that a suitable part of the accounting system has been selected for review.

Once this proposal has been submitted, reviewed and discussed with the assessor then each section of the report should be written. The report should follow the same rules and format required of a student preparing a report based on their own work place. Each section, once completed, should be submitted to the assessor for review and feedback.

The actual case study, for use in an assessment, may be in a slightly different electronic format. They may consist of several documents which link together to provide a scenario. Students will be able to view these documents through a secure electronic platform on the AAT SecureAssess system and also print them if required. Terms and Agreements by the AAT will apply.

> ## WARNING!
>
> Please note that the sample report that follows is only an **example** of how your first submission report should look. The main purpose of this example is to provide a guide to **how a report might be laid out**.
>
> You should follow the guidance given by your Assessment Centre when writing your report, and **under no circumstances** copy the wording from this report. You will need to testify that the report you submit is your own and unaided. **If you**

> submit a report with copied paragraphs from this sample answer your
> training provider could report you to the AAT Conduct and Compliance team.

AUTHENTICITY STATEMENT

This is a witness testimony that states that the work completed, to the writer's best knowledge, is your own, unaided and that the recommendations contained within it have been discussed with your manager/assessor.

It should be completed on headed paper (if completed on own workplace), be signed and dated by your manager/assessor (see below) and have their full contact details.

If you have completed the project by reference to your work place then this statement **must** be completed by your manager and be on your organisation's headed paper. This effectively not only confirms that the work is your own and unaided, but also gives you permission to use your organisation as the basis of the project.

If you have completed the project based on an AAT Case Study then this must be completed by your assessor, on your training organisation's headed paper. In order for them to be able to testify that the work is your own, and unaided, it is essential that you communicate with them throughout the assessment process with project proposals and as per your agreed submission dates on your Assessment Plan.

The Sample Case Study – Cookridge & Cookridge Carpets Ltd

INTERNAL CONTROL & ACCOUNTING SYSTEMS

CASE STUDY

COOKRIDGE & COOKRIDGE CARPETS LIMITED

This sample case study is intended to indicate the type of situation that candidates will be presented with, and as such should be considered as an abridged version of those that will actually be used for live assessments.

COMPANY HISTORY

Cookridge & Cookridge Carpets Ltd is a large carpet, soft furnishings and bed dealership based in Southampton. It is the main dealer for 'Memo@ memory' foam beds and mattresses in the area, and has been trading for the past four years, having been established in 2009. It was set up by two brothers, Peter and John Cookridge.

Peter is a trained carpet fitter, and has been in the soft furnishing industry of the past twenty years. Before going into business with his brother he was the senior manager in a national carpet chain. His brother John, who is three years younger, was recently made redundant from his role as a mining engineer.

They decided to set up the business using John's £80,000 redundancy money and an inheritance the brothers received upon the death of their uncle. Peter had only a small mortgage on his house, and he managed to raise a loan of £100,000 (using the house as collateral) which was also invested in the business.

The brothers purchased a large plot of land on which they developed an aircraft hangar-sized building to use as the carpet and bed showroom. They started out selling carpets, and then expanded into beds and soft furnishings. This expansion was organised by Peter, who had developed excellent working relationships with carpet manufacturers from his time in the industry.

In February 2013 Cookridge & Cookridge Carpets Ltd was asked by Memo Beds to become the main dealership for Southampton, as the existing local dealer was retiring and they wanted a local company to run their franchise. They have been very successful in direct sales, and have recently started selling carpets and beds over the internet. This venture seems to have increased business.

Peter is married to Sasha, who is a teacher in the local primary school for children with special needs. They have twin seventeen year old boys, Mark and Matthew, who are both keen amateur rugby players and play for their local rugby club. Mark is at college studying for his 'A' levels, and Matthew has started a modern apprenticeship in motor engineering in a local garage which is run by a friend of his father. Peter's main hobby, besides watching his sons play rugby at the weekend, is building and racing motorbikes. His is a popular and well-known figure on the local motor racing scene.

John is married to Paula, who acted as company secretary for the first two years of the company's existence. She then left work to have her first baby, who is now nine months old. Paula has now made the decision that she does not want to return to work, preferring to stay at home and be a full time mother.

The business employs twenty staff, composed of:

- Nine direct sales people
- Three internet sales staff
- Two cleaners
- Two car delivery drivers
- One accessories sales person
- Three part-time staff in the small accounts department

You have just been employed as the **Senior Accounts Clerk**, taking over most of Paula's old responsibilities. As the only full-time accounting staff member, you will supervise the running of the accounts office.

The carpet showroom's opening hours are as follows:

- Open seven days a week
- Operates from 9:00 until 21:00, Monday to Saturday

- Operates from 10:00 until 16:00 on Sunday

The accounts department is open from 9am until 17:30pm, Monday to Friday.

The accounts department's office is located on the first floor of the showroom. Access to the office is by a set of stairs at the rear of the building. Toilet facilities for staff and customers are also on the first floor, so the stairs are used by members of the public.

Once on this floor, access to the accounts office is easy because the keypad lock is never used – the accounts staff prefer to keep the door propped open. The accounts office is open plan, with no private working areas.

Both the brothers are key holders for the business. They hold the only full sets of keys, as one of them is always on the premises at close of business to ensure the property is secure. There is an alarm code they set every evening when they lock up.

ACCOUNTS DEPARTMENT STAFF

The current staff in the accounting office are:

SONJA DOUGLAS (WAGES CLERK)

Sonja joined eight months ago. She is Paula's cousin, and joined the company when Paula decided she was not coming back to work. Although Sonja is willing to work some extra hours if required, she does not want to commit herself to any more permanent hours as she would need to rearrange her child care. Sonja gained qualification in payroll four years ago, but has never progressed any further since due to the arrival of her daughter, Betty. She currently works full days on Wednesdays and Thursdays.

STEFAN KALINOWSKI (ACCOUNTS CLERK)

Stefan was employed one year ago. He works four days a week, and has chosen not to work Fridays. This is because his main hobby is music, he plays in a band every weekend and Friday is his rehearsal day. He has had no formal accounting training, but was trained on-the-job in his last role and by Paula before she left the company.

MARGARET PETERSON (ACCOUNTS CLERK)

Margaret joined the company eighteen months ago (application letter on file but no CV). She is employed on a part-time basis of five half days per week, and she likes to work these together to save on her bus fares to work. She currently works all day Tuesday and Wednesday and a half-day on Thursday morning.

The CVs and job descriptions, as displayed on the following pages, are also in Paula's personnel files.

CURRICULUM VITAE

Name: Sonja Douglas

Address: 24 South Street
SOUTHAMPTON
S12 4RT

Email: Sonja@btinternet.co.uk

Mobile: 07792 236543

D.O.B: 2.3.1984

Comments: As a working mother, I am a well organised and competent worker, dedicated to any role I take on.

Education:

2004 – AAT NVQ Level 2 in Payroll gained at Southampton College

2002 – A level maths, grade C; A level general studies, grade A

2000 – 6 GCSEs at grade C and above including maths and English

Employment history:

2004/5 – Arthur C Clarke (engineering factory); trainee payroll clerk

2005/6 – Arthur C Clarke; payroll clerk; reason for leaving: pregnancy

2007/10 – Frescos; evening shelf stacker, reason for leaving: to improve my career prospects now my daughter is in playschool

Hobbies: Swimming; playing with my baby daughter

References: Mr C Hancock, Managing Director, Arthur C Clarke & co

Mrs G Biggs, HR Manager, Frescos

JOB DESCRIPTION

WAGES CLERK

Hours: 15 hours over two full days per week

Salary: To be agreed

Responsibilities:

- To prepare weekly and monthly payroll information. To calculate all monies due (wages and commission) accurately

- To prepare payslips and make up pay packets for the weekly paid staff, and prepare BACS returns for monthly paid staff

- To prepare all associated returns and documentation

- Must be willing to undertake extra hours as needed

Responsible to: The company secretary of the office manager

Responsible for: Self, security of information and security of payroll cash

As this is a new position, other duties may be required on an ad hoc basis.

CURRICULUM VITAE

STEFAN KALINOWSKI

42 St James Avenue
Burnistly
Near Southampton
S25 6RE

30.05.1994

Overview

I left the sixth form of Burnistly Grammar School last year, as I wished to enter the world of work rather than go to university, and would like a career in accounting. I am a bright, capable worker, and am happy to work on my own or as part of a team. I was Head Boy at school, and am happy to take on responsibility.

Last position:

2012 – 2013	Accounts Receivable Clerk – Swannage County Supplies (Company went into administration and I was made redundant)

Education:

2005 – 2012	Burnistly Grammar School
	GCSE Advanced levels Accounting, grade A
	Mathematics, grade C
	Music, grade A*

Aim: To learn more about accounting and to become a qualified accountant.

Hobbies: Music is a passion, both listening to it and playing. I play in a local group.

References:

Mr J Johnson	Mrs C Smith
Accountant	Headteacher
Johnson & Co	Burnistly Grammar School
Eastborough	Hight Road
Swannage	Burnistly

JOB DESCRIPTION

ACCOUNTS RECEIVABLE CLERK (SALES LEDGER)

Hours: 37.5 hours over five days per week

Responsibilities:

- To prepare sales invoices
- To manage credit accounts
- To ensure that all payments are made within 90 days
- To prepare monthly management information
- Must be willing to undertake extra hours as needed

Responsible to: The company secretary of the office manager

Responsible for: Self, security of information and security of cash

Margaret Peterson

10 Mandela Grove

Southampton

S2 4WS

30.06.2012

Dear Sir,

I wish to apply for the position of accounts clerk that was advertised in the Southampton Herald.

I am 57 years old and have recently been widowed. I need to return to work to supplement my income.

I have several years' experience in operating accounting systems, but have not worked in this area for over two years since I left my last role to care for my sick husband. However, though not qualified, I am a competent accounts clerk and references can be obtained from my previous employer, with whom I worked for ten years.

Yours faithfully

M Peterson

M Peterson (Mrs)

JOB DESCRIPTION

ACCOUNTS PAYABLE CLERK (PURCHASE LEDGER)

Hours: 20 hours over five days per week

Responsibilities:

- To check GRN and purchase invoices
- To liaise with carpets, beds and soft furnishing suppliers
- To manage accounts payable accounts
- To ensure that all payments are made accurately and on time
- To prepare monthly management information
- Must be willing to undertake extra hours as needed

Responsible to: The company secretary of the office manager

Responsible for: Self

COOKRIDGE & COOKRIDGE CARPETS (CCL LTD)

MISSION STATEMENT

Our mission is to provide an excellent level of service to all of our customers, whether they are spending £5 or £5,000 – and to provide carpets, beds and soft furnishings that make a house into a home.

We are trying to be a greener company and we recycle wherever possible; we promise to remove all of the packaging from customer's premises, and dispose of this in an environmentally friendly way.

INFORMATION TECHNOLOGY POLICY (JUNE 2010)

All computers can only be accessed by staff who have been authorised by management to use Cookridge & Cookridge Carpets computers. All computers must be password protected.

Computers must only be loaded with licensed software owned by the company. No changes to software are permitted without consent of Cookridge & Cookridge Carpets directors. No member of staff is allowed to load any software onto computers without prior permission from the management.

No unauthorised devises are to be used to saving, uploading or downloading work (eg discs, memory sticks, external hard drives or other devises) other than those purchased and approved by the company.

Computers should only be used for company business and must not be used to access any social networking site.

Staff making unfavourable comments regarding Cookridge & Cookridge Carpets, their management, operating procedures or customers on any social networking site will be deemed to be guilty of spoiling the reputation of the organisation and this will be a disciplinary matter.

Paula Cookridge
Company Secretary

INFORMATION TECHNOLOGY SYSTEMS

There are four computers in the office, as the brothers have provided one for every member of the accounts team.

These are all run on a standalone basis, though they are all linked to the same printer. The inventory information on beds, carpets and soft furnishings is kept on Microsoft Excel spreadsheets. Paula has worked with the software previously, and thought it would be a good idea to set up the company accounting system using the same software.

Three computers were purchased new when the company was established and are running on the Windows 7 operating system; They are also loaded with Microsoft Office 2010 (with a three user licence). Six months ago another new computer was purchased and loaded with Sage Payroll software to enable the payroll to be run in-house. The Microsoft Office package was also installed on this new computer.

When the computer system was set-up a password was set to protect the information stored on it. The password is 'Paula C', and this is used for everything throughout the company because it was set up by Paula when she was company secretary and has never been changed. The idea was that the password would change every three months by having one keyword per computer and then changing the following number. For example, 'Slug1' would then change to 'Slug2' at the beginning of the next quarter, and three months later to 'Slug3', etc.

Paula had also asked everyone in the accounts office to give their computer a password and send it to her, so that she would be able to access all of the computers at any time. However, this was never done.

BPP
LEARNING MEDIA

ACCOUNTS PAYABLE

CARPETS AND SOFT FURNISHINGS

All inventory is purchased on credit terms from a very wide range of suppliers. This is one of Peter Cookridge's roles, and he enjoys spending time researching new inventory lines and new soft furnishing accessories; he also likes meeting the sales staff from different suppliers. He has a favourite group of suppliers he tends to use, mainly because they are sometimes willing to sponsor his motorbike and racing efforts. There is no formal list of suppliers.

All inventory (stock) levels are maintained on the Excel spreadsheets. These have been set up to show:

- Suppliers
- Cost prices
- Selling prices
- Profit margins
- Re-order levels and quantities.

Margaret has worked on Excel previously, but this was over ten years ago. Whilst she is competent at inputting data she sometimes struggles with anything beyond this.

Suppliers are paid at the end of the month in which their invoice is received, as long as funds are available. However, since the recession some suppliers now request payment within thirty days of the date of invoice, and this is beginning to cause John some concern.

Cookridge Carpets holds a large inventory, with many rolls of carpet in the warehouse for sale on a cash and carry basis. Peter has heard that some large companies have recently asked their suppliers to cut the wholesale price by 10%, and is considering approaching two of their largest suppliers to ask them whether this would be a possibility.

All suppliers are paid by cheque. These are completed by Margaret, and then signed by either John or Peter as they are now the only authorised signatories. The cheque book is stored in a locked drawer in Marion's desk in the accounts office.

MEMO BEDS

Memo Beds supply all the memory foam beds to the organisation. These are now the best selling line in beds. They supply products to Cookridge & Cookridge Ltd on a line of credit. The showroom beds are used as demonstration models, and these are paid for 90 days after receipt.

Customers' beds are purchased to order. A minimum deposit of 20% must be made when the order is placed and the rest of the monies are due for payment to the suppliers within 60 days.

Again, all inventory records are stored on Excel spreadsheets. It is the job of the warehouse manager to update the spreadsheets when inventory is delivered into the warehouse, or when inventory is moved from the warehouse into the showroom. This should always be supported by documentary evidence, for example goods received notes (GRNs).

However, on busy days, the warehouse manager will often just update the spreadsheet when sending goods from the warehouse into the showroom, and then ask the sales staff for an inventory requisition note when they are less busy.

ACCOUNTS RECEIVABLE

Stefan is responsible for the running of this function. Whilst some customers do pay cash for their goods, over 60% take extended credit terms. When Stefan first started at Cookridge & Cookridge Carpets, anyone who applied for a credit account was accepted.

However, Stefan realised that this was not good practice and he now uses a credit reference agency to ensure that potential new credit customers have no history of poor payments. Once they this check, any new customer who applies is automatically granted an unlimited line of credit.

All new credit accounts are set up on the first day of the month. Stefan often works extra hours on this day to ensure this task is completed. All sales orders are received by the showroom store staff for processing, and after completion are passed to the accounts department the next morning, so that Stefan can prepare and record the invoices. Stefan has designed a form in Microsoft Word that he uses as a pro forma for invoicing.

To encourage sales, and to compete with large national retailers, Cookridge Carpets offers monthly payment terms to all customers with 6 months interest-free credit. Once this period expires there is an annual interest rate of 28.4%. They finance this through Westbridge Finance, which charges an annual rate of 8.7% to the company.

Stefan is responsible for ensuring payment occurs. The company policy regarding non-payment is as follows:

- Once payment is seven days overdue Stefan will telephone the customer.

- If payment is not received within 14 days of the telephone call, then Stefan writes to the customer requesting payment and for the account to be brought into order.

- If payment is still not received within the next 14 days, the customer's details are passed onto a debt collection agency which works on behalf of the company.

The debt collection agency charges £80 per case, plus 30% of any monies collected. Though this is their policy, the Cookridge brothers this this is a very expensive option, and often do not bother following through with it.

CASH AND BANKING

Cash in

Stefan opens the mail every morning and sorts through it. Any cash or cheques received from customers are entered manually into a day book to record the receipt. The day book is then used to update the ledger accounts, and the cheques and cash are placed in the office safe until a banking day.

At the end of every day, all cash and cheques are removed from the tills, leaving a float of £100 cash in each till for the start of the next day. The principle is that the till should be balanced to ensure that the cash content is correct.

However, during the week this does not happen as the store closes at 21:00, and the sales staff feel that they should not be asked to do an extra job at this hour.

As a result, it is common practice that all cash (except for the till floats) and cheques are removed and bagged as takings from individual tills before being stored in the safe in the accounts office.

Banking

Banking is carried out on a Monday and Thursday, and this is normally Stefan's job which he does during his lunch break.

There is often less cash banked on Thursdays. This is because John and Peter have started to take available cash from the office safe to pay wages in order to reduce the amount of money drawn from the bank via cheques.

Authorised signatories

Any one signature from:

- Peter Cookridge
- John Cookridge
- Paula Cookridge (removed from mandate 30.10.13)

Petty cash

£100 is drawn from the bank every month and placed in a tin. A list of what it is used from is kept in a notebook in the tin, and anyone using the petty cash money is expected to make a note of the date and expense, and sign against this. The tin is kept in the staff room, next to the tea and coffee.

WAGES AND SALARIES

Until six months ago the payroll was completed by the company's accountants, Southampton Accounting Services. Initially Paula was going to run the payroll, but found that this was too demanding of her time and she decided to commission the accountants to perform this task.

However, because the individual hours worked each week by staff (and commissions earned on carpet sales) are so variable, the payroll run is different every week. The accountants charged for the time taken to complete payroll, so it became a costly process for the company.

The brothers decided that wages and salaries could be run internally. For the first two months they used a temping agency, but this was also an expensive option. When Sonja started working for the company eight months ago, she took over payroll duties.

All staff except those in the accounts department are paid weekly in cash. Pay packets are available from the showroom manager, Jim Andrews, from 10:00 on a Friday morning. The rest of the staff are paid monthly, by cheque, on the last working day of each month.

The following table sets out the working hours, rates of pay and frequency of payments for the various categories of staff in the company.

Staff	Rate	Normal time	Time and a half	Double time	Pay period
Sales	£8 per hour	40 hours	Hours over 42 Monday to Saturday	Sunday hours	Weekly
Showroom manager	£9.50 per hour	40 hours	Hours over 42 Monday to Saturday	Sunday hours	Monthly
General staff	£7 per hour	40 hours	Hours over 42 Monday to Saturday	Sunday hours	Weekly
Accounts	£16,000 pro rata	37 and a half hours per week	None – salaried	None – salaried	Monthly

Sales staff earn a commission of 2% on the first £30,000 of sales per month, and 5% on any sales over that figure. John Cookridge is responsible for preparing staff rotas to ensure that there is adequate staff coverage for all opening hours. Most of the sales staff are willing to work overtime, so this does not usually create any problems.

Once the week has finished, the completed rotas are given to Sonja who uses them to calculate the amount of hours that the individual staff have worked.

Sonja prepares the payslips from this information on a Wednesday, calculating manually any overtime payments due, and any Sunday working. From this, she calculates how much cash needs to be drawn from the bank and uses the company cheque book (which is kept locked in Margaret's desk) to prepare a cheque ready for signing.

On a Thursday she then prepares the pay packets, which are stored in the office safe for the showroom manager to collect and to hand out to the staff the following day, though any member of sales staff who is not busy will actually do this. Any pay packets not given out are returned to the office safe and remain there until collected by the relevant member of staff.

Salaried staff are paid monthly on the last working day of the month, and this is done using the Bankers Automated Clearing System (BACS). The BACS information is prepared by the wages clerk, signed by either of the brothers, and needs to be with the bank by the 25th of each month.

Envelopes with payslips are handed to each member of the salaried staff by Sonja on the day they are paid. If a staff member is not available, the envelope is placed in their desk drawer. There are no adjustments to be made to any of the monthly paid staff, as overtime payments are not made to them.

Statutory Sick Pay (SSP) is paid to showroom staff, but the office staff are salaried and are allowed six weeks contractual sick pay per year.

The brothers have always trusted their workforce completely and there is no requirement, or system in place, for either store or office employees to sign in or out when they start or finish work.

DIARY OF EVENTS

AUGUST 2012

Peter had taken Wednesday off to take Mark up to London to a university open day. Mark had just finished college, and was going to have that week off before starting as a temporary staff member in the showroom so that he could learn the family business, even though he was more interested in trying to become a full time rugby player.

Sonja was stood at the printer, complaining that yet again the payslips had jammed the mechanism. She was annoyed because the payslips had to be purchased from Sage, and not only were they very expensive, but she only had enough left for this week and next week's payroll run, and she did not want to have to reorder more before she went on holiday.

When Sonja recovered the payslips from the printer, she realised that half of them were now unusable, and so would have to be destroyed. After dropping them in the bin, she asked Stefan to order more before she reprinted the weekly wages run.

Sonja thought it was just bad luck when a message appeared on her computer to show that the printer ink cartridge needed to be replaced. She was further annoyed because she had asked Stefan to replace this yesterday when he was printing out the invoices, but he had failed to do this. She threw the empty cartridge in the bin before reminding Stefan that it was only fair for him to change the ink when he saw that it was low. All Sonja wanted to do was for the day to finish as she was really annoyed with Stefan, and nothing had gone right for her.

Stefan's music was his main love outside of his work. Whilst he was happy to work longer hours than the other accounting staff, he wanted to keep his Fridays free for music. Peter could see no problem with this, so now Stefan worked flexi-time, arriving an hour before any of the other accounting staff and departing an hour later to make up his hours so that he did not have to work on Fridays.

As Stefan was the first one in the building on Monday morning, he was opening the post and logging cash and cheques that had arrived into the day book, when the telephone rang. It was Margaret to say that she had had a very bad toothache over the weekend, and had an emergency dental appointment for that morning so she would be late for work. Stefan went back to his task of opening the mail, without noticing he had dropped a cheque he was just about to write into the day book behind the desk.

Paula called into the office to show off her baby before she joined John for a family lunch. As she was short on cash and did not have time to go to the bank, she helped herself to £40 from the petty cash tin, and told Stefan that John would replace it this afternoon when he returned from their lunch date.

John was becoming concerned that some customers were becoming increasingly slow in making payments on their credit accounts. He asked Stefan to prepare a schedule of debtors, but Stefan was busy doing invoices and asked if this could be done next month. Stefan has not chased up late payments recently because Paula had said that although she was meant to do this on a weekly basis, she only did it when she had time.

SEPTEMBER 2012

Sonja was going on holiday this month. The last time she went on holiday, she completed two weeks of pay packets on the same date (all based on the hours worked in the week prior to her preparing the wage packets) because she knew that she was the only member of staff who could operate the Sage payroll system. She completed these pay packets and placed them in the safe, informing her supervisors that Stefan would give them out each Friday, and that any over- or under-payments would be adjusted in the following week when she returned to work.

However, there have been mistakes in this process, and it had taken a full month for the resulting errors to be corrected, so Peter had said that she should not do this again. This time, Sonja asked Margaret if she could do the wages run for the weeks of her absence, because she knew that many years ago Margaret used to operate a payroll. Margaret had promised her she would try to do this, but she did not know how to operate Sage. Instead, Margaret said she could prepare the payroll manually using HMRC tax and NI tables, and then Sonja could update the computer system when she came back from holiday.

It was a hot Monday morning and the sales staff complained to Jim Andrews that the milk had gone sour in the refrigerator and they could not have any drinks because of this. Jim sent Kim Lee, a junior member of the sales staff to go to the nearby store and buy 2 litres of milk, telling her to take the money out of the petty cash tin. She returned saying there was no money left in the tin, and so Jim took £10 out of the till and put a note in saying what he had done. When Jim complained to Margaret, she said it was strange because there had been £100 put into the tin a week before, yet on checking the note book there was only £40 spent in the last two weeks.

On the second Tuesday of the month, the bank telephoned to warn the company that as they had reached their overdraft limit they were unable to honour a direct debit due out that day. John said that this was just an oversight and he would deal with it immediately. He emptied the tills and banked £900 in cash so that the direct debit would be covered. He then asked Stefan to produce an aged receivables list so that he could see why the cash flow was so limited when trade had appeared to have picked up. John was disappointed to note that Stefan had not been chasing up debts owed beyond an initial phone call if the debtor stated that they would ensure the payments were brought up to date.

Mark was helping Stefan in the office as part of his summer job. Stefan was busy updating invoices, and thinking that Mark had read all the company policies, he let Mark open two new credit accounts for customers. Mark did this, but without taking any credit references.

On returning from holiday, Sonja was approached by Jo Sellers, one of the sales team. He had been expecting commission totalling £80 in his wages, but Margaret had not allowed for this and had only prepared his wages based on basic hours worked. He told Sonja that he really needed this money, but Sonja knew she could do nothing until the next wages run, and told him so.

Jo was so upset by this that Sonja told him she would borrow the money out of the petty cash tin and replace it when she made his wages up. He was very pleased, and told her that she had made his day, as he had to buy a birthday present for his mother. Sonja was pleased to have helped him, but made a mental note to ask Peter or John if they could provide some training for Margaret so that she could work out the commissions due.

OCTOBER 2012

A new warehouse manager, Joe Bloggins, was employed this month. His last job was at a well-know DIY store, where he was the deputy warehouse manager. The first task he did was to complete an inventory check, and he informed the brothers that there was a shortfall of £3,000 in the actual physical inventory against that on record. He complained to the brothers that there was no evidence of when goods had been taken from the warehouse to the showroom.

Joe also noted that the company they were using to remove waste cardboard and paper were charging per collection, and had started to collect on a weekly basis rather than twice a month as contracted. When he pointed this out to the waste collection service, they informed him that the previous warehouse manager had asked for this increase because there was so much packaging to collect. This had been done without informing the management, whom he knew would be happy to accept this as it was an environmental issue. Joe thought that the brothers should contact the new employer of the previous warehouse manager to inform them that he should have been given a written warning after making contractual changes without the required authorisation.

Stefan went to John to inform him that there was a major supplier account due to be paid and that the overdraft limit would not allow them to draw this cheque. Stefan had checked the invoice, as it was for nearly three times greater than was normal from this supplier, but all seemed to be in order. John did not know why this had happened, but when he asked Peter why he had placed such a large order, Peter informed him that the supplier had promised to sponsor his next motorcycle show if he increased his order.

Peter thought that this would be good business practice and would help increase trade. When John told him that this supplier could not be paid due to poor cash flow, Peter was very annoyed as he did not want to lose the sponsorship. After having an argument over the amount that had been ordered, John then agreed to telephone the bank and explain the situation, and to ask them for an increased overdraft limit for one month only to allow the supplier to be paid.

NOVEMBER 2012

Once again Sonja was complaining that the printer was jammed with payslips, which had meant her throwing away the spoilt payslips for the monthly paid staff. She asked Peter if they could have a new printer, or just print the payslips on plain paper, as she did not have time to align the printer and the payslips correctly.

Joe is also a motorbike fanatic, and on the first weekend of the month he went to a motorbike rally with Peter. Whilst there, he told Peter he was settling in well, but was unhappy with the record keeping system for inventory control. Another error had occurred recently when one of the warehouse staff had entered a delivery incorrectly onto the spreadsheet whilst Joe was on his lunch break. Peter said that as Christmas was approaching they would be very busy, but after Christmas he would review the matter with John and Joe together. The conversation then reverted to the Christmas party, and the subject was never raised again.

Joe Bloggins spoke to Sonja and explained that he had taken on an extra member of staff for the Christmas rush and January sales. He said that the new member would be paid on an hourly rate, and that as he was a student he would not pay tax, and would just need a cash payment weekly. Sonja asked for the new starter document that all new employees had to complete, but Joe had not asked for this to be done, and instead asked Sonja to just add him to the payroll system and he would send through the completed document later on. Sonja agreed, and added new worker A. Lias to the payroll, leaving herself a diary note to ask Joe for the documentation.

DECEMBER 2012

The first weekend was the office Christmas party which was held at the Grand Hotel. They had a great time, especially as the brothers had agreed to pay for the evening and had given everyone a £10 allowance for drinks.

Stefan's brother, Adalbert (known as Addie for short) was home from university for the Christmas holidays. Trade was beginning to increase, and January sales were looming. Stefan had mentioned how busy the showroom staff were, and so Addie asked Peter if there were any holiday jobs available, as he could use the extra money to help fund his next year at university. Peter was happy to employ him for the next six weeks – not in the showroom, but in the warehouse.

It was Stefan's role to prepare invoices and send them to customers. He gathered the information by completing day books from the purchase orders which were written out by the sales staff in the showroom. As Stefan did not work on a Friday, he was always very busy on Monday, as he had invoices from both Friday and Saturday to prepare. However, now that Addie was working, Stefan came up with the idea that Addie could write up the day books from the purchase orders, and this would save him time on a Monday morning.

Addie was also into music, and as he had been working on a voluntary project while at university he discussed with Stefan the possibility of doing some type of community event, based on music, to enhance the lives of children at the nearby school for children with severe learning disabilities (where Sasha worked). Whilst Peter thought this was a good idea, John was not too happy about it, and said that if they wanted to do this they would need to arrange it in their own time, and use their holiday entitlement days for it.

Stefan asked Peter and John if he could start college next month to further his AAT studies on a part-time basis. Both of the brothers thought that this was a good idea, and said that whilst they could not give him any time off to study, they were willing to pay the cost of his course, books and exam fees as long as he guaranteed he would continue to work for them for one year after completing his course. Stefan was happy to do this and signed an agreement to this fact. Peter and John were discussing the importance of training and though they felt that Margaret was probably too old to benefit from this, they decided to offer Sonja training as well with the same conditions. Sonja was not willing to sign an agreement tying her to the company and said she knew her job, and did not need any more training.

Knowing that they were trying to keep receivables more in line with their agreed credit terms, Stefan asked Mark to telephone all customers with outstanding balances. One customer, A. Smith and Jones Ltd, stated that they had paid their account in full by cheque over six weeks ago and were very annoyed that they were now being chased for the money.

CarPet suppliers, one of their major suppliers, have requested urgent payment of an invoice that has been outstanding for 60 days. This invoice was for £30,000 and though this would normally have been paid, there were not enough funds in the bank to cover this amount. When Margaret informed John of this, he was very surprised at the amount of the invoice, and asked her to review all the goods received notes (GRNs) for May to see what carpets had been ordered to cause such a large invoice. Margaret spent a day completing this reconciliation and found that there was an error and they had been charged for 1,000 meters of twisted wilton instead of 100, this having a wholesale price of £16.99 per meter plus VAT.

JANUARY 2013

Paula came to the office on a Tuesday. Her sister had taken the baby out for the day so she had some free time on her hands. The office was busy as Sonja was on holiday, and Paula was happy to help out by answering the telephone and writing some letters. Paula had just made a coffee and came back to Margaret's desk, which is where she was working, when the phone rang. The caller identified himself as John Commins, the boyfriend of Angel, one of the sales staff.

He asked to speak to her, but when Paula checked she discovered that Angel was on holiday that week. John said it was urgent that he spoke with her so Paula gave him Angel's home telephone number and address from Sonja's personnel files.

The bill for the Christmas party was received from the Grand Hotel. It averaged out at £160 per head, including all the drinks and wine. John asked Margaret to put the bill through the company accounts by splitting the bill so that £140 was put through as a tax deductible expense, and the other £20 per head put through as a subsistence claim against expenses. However, Margaret knew the bill came to £160 per head, and that as such it was over the limit of £150 as a legitimate taxable expense, and therefore should not be included. Whilst Margaret was aware that the method John was asking her to use to account for this bill would mean a smaller tax liability, she did not like to do this because it was in breach of current HMRC rules. She did account for the bill by splitting it because she was frightened of what John would say if she did not comply with his wishes.

Peter and John were discussing the possibility of expanding and opening a new showroom in Brighton, about seventy miles away from their current location. They felt that they could run this by just employing one member of staff, managing the new showroom themselves to start with by travelling on a daily basis, and even by asking some of their staff in Southampton to travel across to help out if the Brighton shop got busy. They realised that if they were to do this, they would need to look at the finance options open to them, as they would need to borrow heavily to capitalise this venture.

Peter was very concerned as although trade had picked up throughout the summer, they were still not trading at the same level as they had been last year. John reassured him, saying that by having two branches trade must increase, and that the only problem was that the accounts for this year would not show such a healthy financial position. However, the company only prepared accounts on an annual basis, and had only ever needed to produce these for HMRC, and therefore he could not prove how this year's trading was actually going. He then suggested that the way to maximise their chances of obtaining the required bank borrowing would be to ask Paula to step in and prepare up to date accounts that showed the company in the best possible light by reducing the amount of monies owed to creditors for accounts payable.

Stefan was annoyed when he discovered that one of the credit accounts Mark had opened for I Khan had made no payments against credit given at all so far. This customer had bought £1,000 worth of goods and paid an initial deposit in July but had made no payment since then. When Stefan tracked back through the account he realised that no credit reference agency had been used, so he decided to contact the agency to check on this customer, only to find that he had a very poor credit score.

Addie was due to return to university next month. As his printer was not working at home, and he wanted to download and print his timetables, reading list and course information, he came to the office one evening when he knew Stefan would be on his own to use the printer in the accounts office. Peter was therefore surprised when he walked into the office after returning from a meeting with a supplier to find Addie sat alone at Sonja's computer, using both the computer and the printer. When he asked where Stefan was, Addie replied he had gone into the warehouse because there was a problem with the physical inventory balance not matching up with that on the spreadsheet records.

Mark was tidying up in the office one evening as he waited for his father to come and pick him up. All the staff had gone for the evening, but Peter had promised his son a lift home. He decided to rearrange the furniture and was surprised to discover two cheques behind a desk. One was dated August, and one November. He gave them to his father, who said he did not know where they came from but would bank them the next day.

FEBRUARY 2013

Mark had decided not to go to university but to enter the family business instead. He decided he was going to work in all areas of the business to gain a full understanding of what was happening, and he would particularly like to look at the purchasing of inventory as he felt this could be managed better.

All the temporary staff were now laid off, and Sonja realised that she still had no information regarding A. Lias, the temporary warehouse worker who Joe Bloggins had employed. She tried ringing the mobile phone number Joe had given her for him, but found the number was unattainable.

Once again the company had reached its overdraft limit and the wages needed to be paid. Stefan and Mark started to telephone customers with the largest outstanding overdue balances. When ringing one customer, Mr Smythe in South Havant, Mark was surprised when he said he had dropped £500 in cash into the store four weeks ago. Mr Smythe said he had given it to one of the sales staff, and noted that this was a young man, with curly hair, a description that fitted one of the newer sales staff members. Mark went into the store to ask the manager about this cash, and the manager informed him that he knew nothing about it but would make some enquiries. He then organised a search in the store and three hours later called Mark to say that the money had been found in an envelope with Mr Smythe's name on it in the back of a drawer, but that no one could recall it being handed in to them.

Margaret noticed that there was no petty cash left and they needed some money to buy toilet rolls. Peter took £100 out of his pocket and added it to the tin, as that was all the cash he had with him, but again noted that there were no entries in the petty cash book, just several IOUs in the tin.

John and Peter informed the staff that they would be away for the third week in February, as they were going on a family holiday to celebrate their parents' golden wedding anniversary. Peter was concerned that they would be leaving the staff without any financial resources, so he and John both signed a cheque book containing 30 blank cheques so that any bills could be paid if necessary. They gave this into the care of Margaret who placed this into the top drawer of her desk, and promised it would only be used if necessary.

During this week Jo Sellers came to Sonja and explained that once again the commission he had received was not what he had expected, and he was £65 down. He said he needed this to pay his rent. Sonja didn't think that any mistake had been made, but she said that once again she would advance him, as long as it was repaid from his next commission payment. However, when she went to the petty cash tin, this was empty. She knew, however, that Margaret had a supply of blank cheques, so she used one of these making it out to cash, and went to the bank to withdraw £100 for petty cash, ensuring she noted the advance to Jo in the petty cash book.

ASSESSMENT TASKS

You have recently been employed as Senior Accounts Clerk for Cookridge & Cookridge Carpets. This is a full time position, and the organisation is willing to support you finishing your AAT Level 4 studies by attending evening classes at a local college.

The first job the directors have asked you to do is to review the accounting system, the effectiveness of its internal controls, and whether the culture of the organisation could be improved in terms of working ethically and their environmental sustainability.

You are then asked to make any recommendations for improvements that you feel are necessary. The directors know there are many weaknesses, but are uncertain as to how these should be managed.

To help you in this, they have asked the accounts clerk to prepare some brief information about themselves, an overview of the accounting system, and also a list of events that have occurred over the previous few months. This information can be found in the company diary.

The directors have also suggested you review the following documents:

- www.aat.org.uk/sites/default/files/assets/AAT_Code_of_Professional_Ethics.pdf

- www.aat.org.uk/about-aat/aat-sustainability

You are required to produce a **business report** for Peter and John Cookridge. This should be approximately **4,000 – 5,000** words long.

The report should be mapped to the Internal Controls and Accounting Systems learning outcomes and assessment criteria, by paragraph number, to ensure all criteria are covered.

Task 1

Review and evaluate the accounting system

The review and evaluation can be of the complete system or of one or more of the accounting functions, depending on your findings – but must specifically cover the following areas:

1   Record keeping systems - the purpose of financial reports, and the suitability of the organisation's current reports to meet organisational needs.

2   Internal systems of control – identify how internal control supports the accounting system and the types of internal control in place, and any controls that are missing.

3   Fraud – explain the causes of fraud, common types of fraud, methods used to detect fraud and potential areas for fraud within the organisation.

4   Working methods/practices – review the working methods used, including the use of appropriate computer software, and the operating methods in terms of reliability, speed and cost effectiveness.

5   Training – identify how training is or can be used to support staff.

6   An evaluation of the accounting system's professional ethics against the professional ethics code of the AAT and the organisation; identifying actual or possible breaches of any of the five fundamental principles of the code of professional ethics. Examples of this could include breaches of confidentiality, integrity, professional behaviour, objectivity and professional competence.

7   An evaluation of sustainability within the accounting system, identifying where improvements could be made. This should look at the impact that the organisation has on the environment, the economy or society. Examples of this could be to reduce the carbon footprint, reduce the use of natural resources (paper, electricity, petrol etc) or improving corporate social responsibility.

The review should cover all aspects of the assessment criteria, as mapped above, when it can naturally be introduced into the report. If it cannot be covered in the report then it can be covered within a written explanation included in the appendix.

Whilst a SWOT analysis may be a good starting place and may be referred to in the report, the complete SWOT should not be included in the body of the report.

Task 2

Conduct an ethical evaluation of the accounting system

- Evaluate the accounting system against ethical principles by reviewing working practices

- Identify any actual or possible breaches of professional ethics

Task 3

Conduct a sustainability evaluation of the accounting system

- Evaluate the accounting system against sustainability principles by reviewing working practices

- Identify any possible improvements that could be made to improve sustainability

Task 4

Identify weaknesses and make recommendations for improvement

- Evaluate the system to identify significant weakness, which should be clearly explained along with their impact upon the organisation

- For every weakness that has been identified there should be a recommendation made to attempt to improve the situation

  - The recommendations should concentrate on the effect that the changes would have both on the organisation, and on individual members of staff. They may also highlight training needs or aids to improve staff performance, or changes needed to organisational culture

- Prepare a Cost Benefit Analysis

  - At least one of the recommendations made should be subject to a Cost Benefit Analysis. Whilst not all benefits are quantifiable all costs are, and students should make any necessary assumptions or 'guesstimates' to allocate costs to such items as time, unknown salaries, or any other unknown expense involved in the recommended changes

  - All benefits should be identified, including those which cannot be allocated a financial figure. This can include such things as improved customer relationships, improved documentation systems or staff morale (though this could be allocated a financial benefit as improving staff turnover cuts recruitment costs)

Note on Appendices

Any charts and diagrams or supporting evidence should be included in an appendix and cross-referenced within the text. Any appendices included should be referred to in the main body of the report – or in the case of supporting statements to cover missing assessment criteria, mapped and cross-referenced to a copy of the unit standards.

BPP
LEARNING MEDIA

Sample Report - Cookridge & Cookridge Carpets Ltd

Cookridge & Cookridge Carpets Limited

A report analysing the Internal Controls in place and Evaluating the Accounting system

Student Name:

AAT Registration Number:

I testify that the following report is my own unaided work and a true reflection of the organisation.

Signed: **Dated:**

Contents: **Page No**

Appendices: **Page No**

Word count: 4,253

BPP
LEARNING MEDIA

1. Terms of Reference

1.1. This report investigates the accounting system in place within Cookridge & Cookridge Carpets Limited (Cookridge) with regard to making recommendations to improve the system and the controls in place to protect it - and to reduce the system's exposure to fraud.

1.2. As part of the investigation into the system, this report also looks at the organisation as a whole, and the information the organisation needs from the system. It also investigates the requirements of key stakeholders of the organisation, both internal and external. Ethical and sustainability issues are also considered, and appropriate recommendations for improvements made.

1.3. The report also analyses the recommendations made in terms of their costs and benefits, and analyses the potential for fraud as a risk to the organisation.

1.4. The report has been prepared to cover the requirements of the Internal Controls and Evaluating Accounting Systems Paper that is part of the AAT Level 4 Diploma in Accounting.

2. **Executive Summary**

2.1. This report analyses the internal controls within the accounting system of Cookridge and makes recommendations to improve them. Internal controls can support the accounting function by reducing the risk of fraud and ensuring that accounting system operate appropriately – and that the controls change appropriately as the environment they operate in changes. The main key finding is that a centralised accounting system be installed within the accounts department. The expected cost of the new system is approximately £6,000. Other key recommendations are that the accounts team be trained to use the new system, and that procedural manuals and contingency plans be completed to enable staff to cover absence. A full Cost Benefit Analysis of all the recommendations is included in section 11 of this report.

2.2. Implementing the recommendations made in this report will significantly improve the reporting of the organisation's finances, and this in turn will improve the credit control function, payments to suppliers and relations with them, staff development (and potentially wages) and morale. It will also improve controls and reduce the risk of fraud.

2.3. The report also recommends that the new system be complemented by expanded use of the BACS payments system, so that suppliers and employees are paid direct into their accounts, reducing the use of cash and cheques hence improving controls.

3. **Methodology**

3.1. The information sources used and research performed to produce this report are listed below.

3.2. Research was performed using reference books and the Internet.

3.3. A questionnaire was sent to the internal stakeholders to see what information they required from the accounts department and whether this information was being received in a timely manner.

3.4. The existing accounting system was reviewed over a period of three months to enable a SWOT analysis to be produced.

3.5. A fraud matrix was prepared to investigate the potential of fraud within the accounting system and to analyse the controls in place to prevent them.

3.6. An ethical review of the accounting system was carried out to ensure the business is being carried out with the AAT Code and the five fundamental principles of ethical conduct.

3.7. A sustainability review of the accounting system was carried out against sustainability principles including social, corporate and environmental issues.

4. **Introduction to the Organisation**

4.1. Cookridge is a large, owner run carpet, soft furnishings and bed dealership in Southampton. It is a limited company, set up four years ago by the Directors of the company who employ 17 staff in the stores and one full time and three part time staff in a small accounts department.

4.2. Cookridge has grown since its set up as a carpet business and has since expanded into beds and soft furnishings. It has recently brought the completion of the weekly and monthly wages and salaries in-house, where previously it was completed by a third party organisation. It has also recently employed the fourth member of the accounts team – a Senior Accounts Clerk, a role which includes the managing of the accounts department and the personnel within it.

4.3. The organisation has a relatively flat structure, as shown by the Organisation Chart which is included as Appendix 1 to this report.

4.4. The accounts system in use is a decentralised system consisting of four stand alone computers. The inventory control system is based around an Excel spreadsheet and the payroll system is run using Sage Payroll software. A simple, predictable password is used widely across the company.

4.5. **External regulations affecting the organisation:**

4.5.1. The Companies Act 2006 – this sets out the way in which financial statements should be prepared.

4.5.2. UK Accounting Standards – these further define the policies and approaches to the preparation of accounting statements that the organisation must take. They are either known as Statements of Standard Accounting Practices (SSAPs) or Financial Reporting Standards (FRSs) depending on when they were issued.

4.5.3. International regulations such as International Accounting Standards (IASs) and International Financial Reporting Standards (IFRSs), issued by the International Accounting Standards Board (IASB).

4.5.4. The Data Protection Act 1998 – This regulates how the organisation processes and stores sensitive information on customers, suppliers and employees. Cookridge will need to ensure its systems are compliant with the Act or risk heavy penalties if data is found to be misused and/or stolen.

4.5.5. Late payment law – as set out in the Late Payment of Commercial Debt (Interest) Act 1998 the organisation will need to ensure that it does not delay payments to suppliers beyond acceptable periods.

4.5.6. Health and safety legislation – as set out in a variety of legislation. Cookridge will need to comply with various health and safety principles and policies including having nominated and trained first aiders and safe working practices for staff.

4.6. Cookridge – key external stakeholders

4.6.1. Customers – the customers of Cookridge are individuals who are looking to purchase new carpets, beds or soft furnishings for their home. Their primary concern will be that they are provided with good products and a good service at a reasonable cost. They will also be interested in good credit terms with the organisation. Financial information required will include price lists, as well as information on the credit limit granted to them and also statements regarding how much they owe.

4.6.2. Suppliers – the main suppliers to Cookridge will be the manufacturers or importers of the goods it sells on to customers. These goods will include carpets, beds and soft furnishings. Suppliers will be concerned with prompt payments for the goods supplied. Financial information required will include information to enable them to decide whether to provide credit to Cookridge.

4.6.3. Bank manager – the bank of Cookridge is a key stakeholder as the organisation currently makes heavy use of its overdraft facility. If the overdraft has to be repaid, then this will affect the cash flow of the organisation and potentially its ability to continue as a going concern. The bank will require Cookridge's financial accounts. In particular, it might request to see an accurate cash flow statement to enable them to see that the overdraft can be reduced within the timescale set.

4.7. Cookridge – key internal stakeholders

4.7.1. The Directors – as the owners of the business they will have a key interest in its success and will require various types of information including the final accounts. They will be concerned with the profit of the organisation, looking at turnover and also costs.

5. **The accounts department**

5.1. Cookridge has an accounts team that are situated on the first floor, above the showroom. There is open access to the floor as it also contains toilets used by customers. There is keypad access to the office itself, using a common code in use throughout the organisation. However, the keypad lock is never used as the accounts staff prefer to keep the door propped open.

5.2. All staff working within the organisation can access the office and do so to liaise with the accounting team, for example sales staff that wish to query their wages, and the Directors to discuss the accounts or to sign cheques.

5.3. The purpose of the accounts department is to complete all activities relating to the production of the accounts including sales and purchase ledger and payroll. Due to some of the identified weaknesses there is little management accounting activity or cash flow forecasting. An organisation chart is included in Appendix 1.

5.4. **The accounts department – key internal stakeholders**

5.4.1 Wages Clerk – responsible for the preparation of the wages and salaries of staff. The clerk works two days per week and has an NVQ 2 in payroll.

5.4.2 Accounts Clerk 1 – the accounts clerk responsible for accounts receivable (sales ledger) runs all trade credit accounts for the organisation, working full time hours condensed into four days per week. The clerk has an A level in Accounting but no formal training and was trained on the job by the previous clerk.

5.4.3 Accounts Clerk 2 – the accounts clerk responsible for accounts payable (purchase ledger) works five half days per week. The clerk has several years experience in operating accounting system but this was ten years ago. The clerk is relatively new to this role.

5.4.4 Senior Accounts Clerk – the recently-appointed Senior Accounts Clerk is responsible for managing the accounting team and systems and producing this report investigating the weaknesses of the accounts systems, with a focus on the payroll system, and making recommendations to improve them.

5.4.6. Other staff – Cookridge staff outside the accounts department include salespeople, cleaners and delivery drivers. Cookridge staff are key stakeholders of the accounts department. They are primarily interested in good working conditions and pay. They need to be paid the correct amount, on time. This requires an efficient, adequately controlled payroll system. Other staff also require accurate inventory information from the accounts team.

6. **Review of the accounting system**

6.1. This report analyses the accounting system in place within Cookridge and makes recommendations to improve it.

6.2. The weaknesses have been identified with the aid of a SWOT analysis – see Appendix 2. This section of the report documents an investigation of the system and consideration of the information the accounts system should provide to stakeholders. It also considers whether the system is suitable to meet stakeholder needs, and the organisation's needs.

6.3. **Working methods and practices**

6.3.1.   The IT systems in Cookridge's accounts department consist of four stand alone computers, each operating independently of each other. The accounting and inventory system use spreadsheet software (Excel), and the payroll system uses Sage Payroll. Invoices to customers are completed using word-processing software (Word).

6.3.2.   Computer files are, in theory, password protected, although the same password is used across the organisation.

6.3.3.   Weaknesses in the working methods and practices within the systems at Cookridge are detailed in the SWOT analysis in Appendix 2. The main points from this are:

- There is a lack of communication. Most staff are part time and some rarely see each other. This can lead to a lack of communication and inefficiencies if they are trying to complete each other's work.

- The separate, independent systems have contributed to the lack of cover across roles within the organisation.

- There is no centralised reporting due to the separate systems in use – this has led to an incomplete picture on the financial position of the organisation, especially in relation to cash flow.

- Many of the current working methods are manual, even more so if a staff member is absent and another person steps in. This could lead to errors.

- The current systems are slow for staff to use. Also, some staff are not fully trained, so are inefficient. The use of Excel and Word provides flexibility but the lack of controls in these general purpose software applications increases the potential for errors.

- There is no back-up taken of the system, putting the organisation at risk of losing key data if the systems failed.

- There is a lack of work planning which could lead to inefficient working, bottlenecks, errors and inconsistencies.

6.4. Record keeping systems

6.4.1. Weaknesses in the record keeping system were identified as part of the SWOT analysis in Appendix 2, the main points include:

- There is no cover for staff when absent leading to urgent work being completed manually and computerised records not being updated.

- Gross pay is calculated manually, which increases the risk of errors.

- A reliance on Excel and Word for record keeping, especially with untrained staff, can lead to errors and inefficiencies. Few staff have the Excel skills required. Errors built in to the spreadsheet could go unnoticed.

- Petty cash is not recorded correctly and cash is taken from tills.

- When the tills are closed at the end of the day there is no recording of balances of cash/cheques etc.

- Wages have been completed in advance and therefore were not accurate.

- Errors in wages have been corrected via a cash advance borrowed from the petty cash tin.

- Cheque use is not recorded, there are incomplete records as to what they have been used for.

6.5. Training

6.5.1. The SWOT analysis in Appendix 2 analyses the weaknesses within the system with regards to training, the main points include:

- Staff lack accounting knowledge and training. As a result, there are inadequate general controls and procedures, and a lack of responsibility taken for their work.

- Staff have not received training in the systems used, for example the Excel pivot tables. This increases the risk of error.

- Staff have not been made aware of the ethical principles to which the business should adhere (see Appendix 4). One example is the failure to maintain confidentiality.

- Staff have not been made aware of the importance of sustainability in the operations of the business. Ink cartridges are not recycled and paper is wasted.

7. Ethical evaluation of the Accounting System

7.1. An ethical review of the Accounting System identifying potential breaches and recommending best practice has been completed. The findings are shown in Appendix 4. In summary, the issues include:

7.1.1. Personal details of a member of staff have been given out without the permission of the employee, a breach of ethics and of data protection.

7.1.2. HMRC tax regulations have been breached by splitting payments to get around tax deductible expense limits.

7.1.3. Misleading accounts have been prepared in order to secure a bank loan, a deceitful unethical and fraudulent action.

7.1.4. The company has a Microsoft Office user license for three users, however, this is used by four users.

8. **Sustainability review of the Accounting System**

8.1. Appendix 5 shows the findings from a sustainability review of the Accounting System. It finds that:

8.1.1. Cookridge addresses environmental issues in its mission statement. However, this statement needs to be backed up by policies and procedures that are implemented at the operational level.

8.1.2. Ink cartridges are currently not recycled.

8.1.3. Paper (particularly payslip paper) is wasted.

9. Internal controls and analysis of fraud

9.1. Internal systems of control

9.1.1.   Within Cookridge controls are very informal. Reliance is often based on trust. Formal internal controls would support the accounting system and reduce the possibility of fraud occurring.

9.1.2.   The SWOT analysis in Appendix 2 analyses the internal control and fraud weaknesses. The main points are:

- Cash – there are few controls regarding the use of cash within the organisation. Tills are not counted, cash is used to pay wages, there is no double check of the wages when completed.

- Cheques – controls are inadequate and ineffective, for example the desk drawer where the cheque book is kept has been found unlocked. Blank cheques are also signed and left with staff.

- Authorisation – there are no authorisation procedures in place. All cheques have to be signed by one of the Directors – as a consequence blank signed cheques are left when they are absent. Wages are not authorised effectively and are calculated from unchecked staff rotas.

- Counter-signatures – cash wages are not double checked and countersigned to prevent errors/fraud.

- Passwords/access – one common password is used throughout the organisation including access to the accounts office and systems. Any member of staff could use this password.

- Credit control – the only current control in respect of granting credit to customers is to check with a credit reference agency, however, it was found that in some cases even this was not done.

- New suppliers/customers – there are no controls in place before new suppliers and customers are added to the systems.

- Amendments to contracts with existing suppliers – there are no controls or authorisation processes in place for the amendment of existing contracts.

- Petty cash – no control system is in place.

- Debt recovery – while a relationship with a debt collection agency is in place, this is rarely used due to the costs involved. The debt collection procedures beyond an initial phone call are also often not followed. This may mean that debts are never recovered.

9.2. Analysis of fraud

9.2.1.   There are many possible frauds that could occur within the system at Cookridge and appropriate controls should be in place to prevent them.

9.2.2.   The SWOT analysis in Appendix 2 analyses the weaknesses with the system as:

- The use of cash to pay wages could lead to the theft of cash.

- The use of cash to pay wages could lead to the payroll staff colluding with weekly staff and adding more cash to the pay packet than the amount earned or shown on the wages slip.

- Cheques are not stored securely, so could be stolen and used fraudulently.

- Cheques are signed and left blank for staff to use when the owner is absent. This increases the risk of fraudulent use.

- There are no controls re new suppliers and so staff could defraud the organisation by setting up a bogus supplier and making payments to it.

- There are no controls re new customers and so staff could defraud the organisation by setting up a bogus customer.

- There are no controls over the set up of new employees which could lead to the set up of ghost employees for personal gain.

9.2.3.   Each of these potential frauds, the current controls in place, and the recommendations to improve can be found within a fraud matrix in Appendix 3. This matrix also includes the level of risk to the organisation.

10. Recommendations to improve

10.1.   There are many recommendations that can be implemented to improve the weaknesses identified above and in Appendix 2.

10.1.1.   The first is that a centralised, integrated accounts package be purchased. This will need the computers currently in use within the department to be networked, so all staff access the same files. This would enable the organisation to have central, integrated accounting records. Staff morale and motivation should improve, as they will be learning new skills, using an effective system and be provided with appropriate information. The reduction in manual calculations would lead to fewer errors, benefiting both staff and the organisation.

10.1.2.   Staff must be fully trained to use the system so that they can operate it effectively and efficiently. This will improve their productivity and morale.

10.1.3.   The system should also be properly backed-up with procedures detailing who is responsible for completing this at the end of each working day. This will ensure the organisation does not lose key information in the event of a system failure.

10.1.4.   Staff should also receive formal accounting training. This will show them they are valued, make them more effective, motivate them and provide them with a much better understanding of the need for appropriate controls. This will in turn benefit the organisation.

10.1.5.   There should also be a review of staff hours and days to ensure that staff are in at appropriate times plus a formal procedure in place to train staff in second roles to cover for each other's absence. This will improve morale as staff are better trained and have more variety in their work plus benefit Cookridge as there will be appropriate cover in place.

10.1.6.   This could be strengthened by the completion of procedural manuals to explain how to operate the systems. This will aid the department In the event of training new staff if required.

10.1.7.   The office door must be kept closed at all times and an effective access code used. All staff must be informed of the need to control access to the accounts office. This will reduce the risk of unauthorised access and fraud.

10.1.8.   Passwords to access the computer system must be robust and changed regularly. Passwords should:

- Not contain the name of any user or use numbers or special characters to get around this

- Be at least 8 characters long

- Contain at least one number, one uppercase letter, one lowercase letter and one special character (eg @#%)

- Be changed every three months

- The controls should prevent the re-use of any password that has been used within the last year

This will reduce the risk of unauthorised access and fraud.

10.1.9.   As part of the centralised accounts system, the use of the BACS payments system should be expanded so that suppliers and staff wages are paid direct into bank accounts, reducing the use of cash and cheques. This will significantly reduce the risk of fraud together with the risk of theft of cash and errors in calculations.

10.1.10. An effective petty cash system should be implemented and petty cash recorded appropriately. This will benefit the organisation by reducing the risk of theft and of inadequate record keeping, for example of cash taken from the tills.

10.1.11. All tills must be counted and reconciled at the end of each working day – staff should be paid to stay back and complete this work. This will reduce the risk of fraud and of errors, and make store staff more accountable for the contents of their till. The culture must move towards one of controls and accountability.

10.1.12. There should be controls in place to add new suppliers and customers to the accounts system, with authorisation only from a Director and/or the Senior Accounts Clerk.

10.1.13. The cheque book should be kept locked in the safe and the system of signing blank cheques stopped. The Senior Accounts Clerk could be added as a second signatory if required. This will ensure staff are happy that they can have cheques authorised in the event of the Directors' absence but benefit Cookridge by reducing the risk of fraud.

10.1.14. Further checks on customers should be completed before they are granted credit. This will benefit the organisation by reducing the risk of bad debts and ensuring that credit is only granted to customers who are likely to be able to pay their debts.

10.1.15. The centralised accounts system will enable full financial reports to be produced, enabling both the owner and the senior accounts clerk to review all aspects of the organisation's financial position. This will ensure better planning of cash flows so that the current overdraft can be reduced and aged debts dealt with appropriately. It will also ensure that suppliers are paid promptly. This will reduce the risk of Cookridge violating their agreed credit terms and being placed on 'stop' due to unpaid bills.

10.1.16. New employees should only be set up on the payroll system upon receipt of specified documentary evidence. It should not be possible to override this requirement. An authorisation procedure should also be required to change the details of existing employees.

10.1.17 It is also recommended that the Senior Accounts Clerk be responsible for the operation and management of the new system, including the setting of appropriate password controls.

10.1.18 A process of checking and authorisation should be set up to ensure that a new starter can only be paid following authorisation from the Senior Accounts Clerk. This should be done via a separate log in to the payroll system.

10.1.19 Regular checks should be carried out of the payroll records against the HR records and vice versa.

10.1.20 A list of preferred suppliers should be established. Selection should be based on commercial criteria including price, reliability and quality.

10.1.21 A formal tender process should be set up for large contracts.

10.1.22 When sourcing new items (for which there is no existing approved supplier) a minimum of three quotes should be obtained. The company that provides the best value for money, taking in to account price, quality and other relevant factors should be selected (this may not necessarily be the cheapest potential supplier, although it may be).

11. Cost Benefit Analysis

11.1. A Cost Benefit Analysis of the recommendation to implement a centralised accounting system, and train staff appropriately on it, has been completed as follows:

11.2. **Costs**

11.2.1. An example of a system that would suit Cookridge's needs is a centralised accounting software package such as *Sage Accounts Professional* - which has been specifically created for small to medium sized organisations. There are many similar packages on the market and a full investigation should be completed to determine which bests suits the organisation. A reputable, proven package with a multi user licence would cost approximately £2,400. The basis for choosing the package should include ease-of-use (for example drop-down menus), the Help facility and the user manuals.

11.2.2. Cookridge would also need to purchase an appropriate support package to ensure users have access to trained support professionals and that software upgrades and bug fixes are received. An estimated cost for this, an additional £1,000 per year.

11.2.3. Appropriate training for staff is required. If the accounts package purchased is one in common use then Cookridge will be able to purchase places on open courses for staff, costing approximately £300 – £500 per staff member. Cookridge might also consider a tailored training course for all staff at once, to include partial set up of the system for Cookridge's use, which would cost approximately £2,000.

11.2.4. There would also be an opportunity cost of the staff attending the training in that they would not be available to complete their work at Cookridge.

11.2.5. The organisation also requires the appropriate equipment to network the computers and this could be completed either by cable or on a secure wireless network, and cost approximately £500 – £1,500. Cabling would be more reliable but create disruption to the office whilst being installed, where as a wireless network would be less disruptive to install, but may be less reliable.

11.2.6. Cookridge would face some disruption whilst the system is installed and set up. There will be a need to pay for additional staff time to enter data on customers, suppliers and employees into the system so that it is fully operational and it is anticipated that this could be completed within one week. This would require an additional 50 paid hours costing approximately £900.

11.2.7. A further cost the organisation should consider, but one harder to quantify, is that of staff discontent at a change to the current system. Staff within the accounts team may be unhappy about needing to learn new working practices, increased controls and how to operate a new system. Other employees may see the increased controls in place as preventing them carrying out their work and unnecessary.

11.2.8. There would be a cost associated with producing procedure manuals to ensure staff know the expected working practices and procedures surrounding the system. There should also be a rota produced for cover, when staff are absent. This should be completed by the senior accounts clerk, as part of their normal role. At an estimate, this would take approximately 20 hours of their time per year.

11.3. Benefits

11.3.1. The first benefit to Cookridge would be the ability to produce reports from the centralised system that provide complete information that shows the full financial position of the organisation. These reports can be reviewed on a regular basis by both the Directors and the senior accounts clerk. The cash related reports should help ensure cash flows are effectively managed. This will benefit the organisation by reducing overdraft fees. The reports produced would include:

- Income statement (profit and loss account)
- Statement of financial position (balance sheet)
- Aged debt analysis
- Cash flow forecast
- Supplier payment reports
- Costs by cost centre/code
- Analysis of petty cash expenditure
- Payroll reports

11.3.3.   An aged debt report can be produced to strengthen the system of chasing overdue debts and ensuring customers who have not paid are put on stop quickly. This will prevent customers from taking advantage of the current lax controls. It has been calculated that approximately £2,000 per year of bad debts would be saved.

11.3.4.   Cash flow forecasts will enable the Directors and senior accounts clerk to estimate the cash inflows and outflows to the organisation, manage cash balances more effectively and reduce the overdraft and related fees. It will also assist with the planning of any significant cash expenditure. Overdraft fees and interest payment could be reduced by up to £3,000 per year.

11.3.5.   The payroll will be accurately produced when required, with the benefit of the system being up to date on payroll rules and regulations such as tax rates. This will produce a benefit of more accuracy, fewer queries and increased efficiency of staff time. It is estimated that the system will speed up the completion of the payroll by approximately 4 hours per month.

11.3.6.   There will be less danger from a system breakdown with appropriate back up of a central system. If one computer were to fail then the other staff could continue working and a support agreement would ensure that if the main system failed it could be operational again as quickly as possible with less risk of lost or corrupted data.

11.3.7.   Another benefit would be improved supplier relations – reports on supplier payments due could be run and suppliers paid on time. This could also benefit the credit terms and conditions that suppliers grant Cookridge, further improving cash flow.

11.3.8.   A further benefit is the significant reduction in the risk of fraud and improvement of controls within the system together with improved cost control. Central reports will assist both the owner and the senior accounts clerk with analysing payments and wages and identifying where costs are higher than expected. Due to current poor controls it is not known if Cookridge has suffered from fraudulent activities so benefits are hard to evaluate.

11.3.9.   A benefit would also be improved morale of staff. The accounts team would benefit from training, including formal accounts training as requested and this would improve their efficiency and effectiveness as well as morale. Better motivated staff should result in lower staff turnover and also improved commitment to the organisation.

11.3.10. The morale of the non-accounting staff would be improved by the timely completion of accurate wages.

11.3.11. A final benefit would be that Cookridge would then be able to comply with regulations such as the Data Protection Act 1998 with good, secure storage of its data and information.

Appendix 1 – Organisation Chart

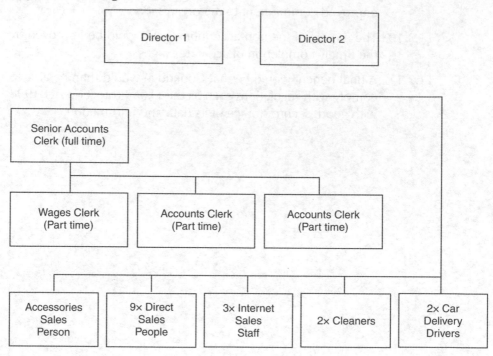

Appendix 2 – SWOT Analysis

Strengths	Weaknesses
▪ An open plan accounts office ensures that when staff are in and working with each other they can communicate freely and cover each other's work when absent. ▪ The cheque book is kept in a locked desk in the office – but see weaknesses. ▪ Current inventory system has good detail included. ▪ Credit reference agency used to decide whether to grant credit. ▪ Some credit control procedures are in place. ▪ Controls re: cash and cheques coming into the office – manual day book then accounts. ▪ Staff seem keen to improve systems – Accounts receivable clerk has implemented some initiatives. ▪ Cash movement is reduced by using cash to make up wages.	▪ As most accounts staff are part time there are often occasions when no one is in the office. The door is generally propped open, there is a risk members of the public could access the office. ▪ As all staff can access the office and the accounts system with common passwords, there is a lack of control. There will also be issues concerning communication between staff as they are not all in the office at the same time. ▪ Stand-alone computers, with no central system or database, reduces the ability to produce meaningful reports for key stakeholders. ▪ Staff, as a whole, are not qualified in accounting which poses a risk of errors and relaxed controls and also a lack of accountability. ▪ There appears to be a lack of planning in the work of the accounting team, highlighted by the fact that when the payroll was first brought in house a temping agency was contracted to run it for the first two months. This could have led to errors and inconsistencies in the work, and the hand over of the system to the payroll clerk once employed. ▪ Stores staff are paid in cash which poses a risk of theft. ▪ Office staff are paid by cheque – the frequent use of cheques can lead to the risk of cheques being stolen and fraudulently used. ▪ Manual calculation of weekly payroll with no secondary check is a weakness as it can lead to errors or fraudulent increases in staff pay.

Strengths	Weaknesses
	▪ Wages are paid in cash – any use of cash poses a risk of theft.
	▪ Debts are often not followed up further to the initial phone call.
	▪ The cheque book is kept in an easily accessible drawer that is sometimes left unlocked.
	▪ Staff are not trained in Excel, increasing the risk of errors.
	▪ New credit customers are not given a realistic credit limit.
	▪ Invoices are produced using Word, has potential for errors.
	▪ Cash is not counted when removed from the tills on weekdays.
	▪ No controls over petty cash and over cash taken from tills.
	▪ No contingency planning – staff able to take on each other's roles when absent.
	▪ Staff are unable to cover each other's roles as they lack the skills to do so.
	▪ No control on authorisation – signing of blank cheques to cover absence.
	▪ No controls on payments to customers.
	▪ Payments to suppliers are made without checking systems, or informing other staff.
	▪ Lack of controls on staff hours have led to incorrect rotas and staff pay.
	▪ Three weeks pay packets completed in one go – this is a weakness as too much cash was in the office.
	▪ Wages should be completed correctly each week, not in advance and adjusted later.

Opportunities	Threats
• There is an opportunity to use one central accounts system on networked computers which will ensure that there is better cover for work when staff are absent and better reporting of key financial data to relevant stakeholders. • There is an opportunity to train staff in accounting and also in the systems they use, making them much more aware of the controls and procedures they should be operating with and also more efficient. • There is an opportunity to train staff in each other's roles – perhaps with a back-up member of staff for each. This could motivate staff and also ensure cover during absence. • There is an opportunity to outsource the payroll and internal audit functions to the company accountants.	• Using spreadsheet software (Excel) to prepare accounts poses a risk of errors being made in formulas that are difficult to spot, resulting in incorrect inventory and accounting information. • The use of one common password is a threat to systems and the data held within them (for example through unauthorised access). • The lack of formal procedures and controls has contributed to the extensive use of the overdraft facility and caused the bank concern. This is a cash flow threat to the organisation. • There appears to be no back-up taken of the current systems. This is a threat, if the systems failed key financial data would be lost. • Regulatory environment – this is constantly changing, for example potential changes to VAT rates. The accounting system needs to recognise these changes and react accordingly. • Debt collection – while a relationship with a debt collection agency is in place, this is rarely used due to the costs involved. This may mean that debts are never recovered.

Appendix 3 – Fraud Matrix

Potential fraud	Current control	Risk to the organisation	Recommendation
The use of cash to pay wages could lead to the theft of cash.	Cash is kept in the safe	5 – High	Pay staff by BACS reducing the use of cash.
The use of cash to pay wages could lead to the payroll staff colluding with weekly staff and adding more cash to the pay packet than earned and on the wages slip.	None – wages are not double checked or countersigned	5 – High	Either ensure a thorough check of wages calculated and cash included or pay staff by BACS as above.
Cheques are not stored securely, so could be stolen and used fraudulently.	Stored in locked drawer – but often found to be unlocked	4 – High	Store cheques in the safe only.
Cheques are signed and left blank for staff to use when the owners are absent. This increases the risk of fraudulent use.	None	5 – High	Allow a second signatory for when absent and reduce use of cheques through BACS wages and payments.
There are no controls re new suppliers and so staff could defraud the organisation by setting up a bogus supplier and making payments to it.	None	3 – Medium	All new suppliers and customers should be entered to a central accounting system and authorised either by owner or senior accounts clerk.
There are no controls re new customers and so staff could defraud the organisation by setting up a bogus customer and purchasing goods from it.	None	3 – Medium	All new suppliers and customers should be entered to a central accounting system and authorised either by owner or senior accounts clerk.

Potential fraud	Current control	Risk to the organisation	Recommendation
There are no controls over the set up of new employees which could lead to the set up of ghost employees for personal gain.	Documentary evidence should be received but the system does not enforce this	4 – High	New employees should only be set up on the system upon receipt of documentary evidence. It should not be possible to override this requirement. Set up a process of checking and authorisation so that a new starter can only be paid once the new starter and the supporting evidence have been checked and authorised by the senior accounts clerk. This should be done via a separate log in to the Payroll system. Carry our regular checks of the Payroll records against the HR system and vice versa.

Key to risk
1 = Low, 3 = Medium, 5 = High

Appendix 4 – Ethical Review of the Accounting System

CURRENT PRACTICE	PRINCIPLE BREACHED AND DETAILS	RECOMMENDED PRACTICE
Disclosure of personal details (address and telephone number) of a member of staff to an individual on the telephone	**CONFIDENTIALITY** There is a requirement to, in accordance with the law, respect the confidentiality of information acquired as a result of professional and business relationships and not disclose such information to third parties without proper and specific authority unless there is a legal or professional right or duty to disclose	▪ Personal details of staff should be stored in accordance with the Data Protection Act and not disclosed without the permission of the employee in question, or unless there is a legal or professional right or duty to disclose
Christmas party bill was split in order to get around HMRC tax deductable expense limits	**PROFESSIONAL BEHAVIOUR** By asking the Payroll Clerk to breach HMRC rules in relation to the bill for the Christmas party, the Director has failed to comply with relevant laws and regulations. By failing to confront the Director rather than carrying out the request, the Payroll Clerk has assisted the Director in breaching this principle	▪ The full £160 does not qualify as a tax deductable expense and as such should not be treated as one ▪ HMRC rules should be fully complied with at all times
A Director asked a member of staff to produce a set of accounts that show the company in the 'best possible light' in order to secure a bank loan	**INTEGRITY** Producing accounts designed to mislead the bank as to the position of the company represents a lack of honesty. To comply with the	▪ Accounts should be prepared that show the company in a true and fair light

CURRENT PRACTICE	PRINCIPLE BREACHED AND DETAILS	RECOMMENDED PRACTICE
	fundamental principle of integrity, a member must be straightforward and honest in all professional and business relationships	
A Director placed an exceptionally large order with a supplier on the basis that the supplier had promised to sponsor a motorcycle show if the order was increased. The Director has a favourite group of suppliers, mainly because they are sometimes willing to sponsor his motorbike and racing efforts	OBJECTIVITY A member shall not allow bias, conflict of interest or undue influence of others to override professional or business relationships. The Director is allowing conflict of interest to affect his professional relationship and judgment. Suppliers should be selected based on the value for money they can offer, not those that offer personal favours in exchange for the business	A formal approved supplier list should be established. ■ Where an approved supplier is not in place, a minimum of three quotes should be obtained and the supplier that offers the best value for money should be chosen

Appendix 5 – Sustainability Review of the Accounting System

Sustainability issue	Observation	Recommendations
Corporate social responsibility/ environmental	Cookridge's mission statement states that 'we are trying to be a greener company and we recycle wherever possible; we promise to remove all of the packaging from customers' premises, and dispose this in an environmentally friendly way'	This mission should be supported by a series of objectives, policies and procedures to ensure this happens in practice
Environmental	Used ink cartridges are placed in the bin when they are removed from the printer	These items may need to be disposed of in a specific way due to the chemicals involved. Many types of ink cartridge can be recycled. This should be done if possible

Appendix 6 – Technical Notes

If an assessment criterion is not covered in the report (or not to the depth required by the assessor), then this can be covered within a written explanation included in the appendix.

Where this is the case technical notes should be included in the appendices to the report to ensure that an area of the standards is covered in sufficient detail to clearly demonstrate competence.

Exactly what will be required by the technical notes will depend on every student and assessor plus the workplace vs. case study used to complete the report.

It should be noted that as these notes are in the appendices they do not contribute to the word count.

In the example of Cookridge examples of appropriate technical notes might include:

1   **Statement of profit or loss** – In the context of Cookridge this would show the Directors of the organisation the income or revenue received and the costs of the business. This could show profitability by month or by product depending on the detail required. This would assist the Directors with making decisions and analysing the business and would highlight key costs such as bank interest. This would have led to an earlier understanding of the size of the overdraft. Once costs like these have been identified they then can be better controlled.

2   **Statement of financial position** – In the context of Cookridge this would show the assets and the liabilities of the organisation. It would also show details of the receivables (debtors) and payables (creditors) and allow the owner to have a regular and more accurate picture of these. This would help to highlight any issues with the size and/or management of payables and receivables.

3   **Cash flow forecast** – This is often required by a bank when deciding whether to grant a loan or extend an overdraft. The Directors of Cookridge will prepare a report, probably on a spreadsheet, showing cash expected to be received and paid out each month over the next 6-12 months. The will show the expected balance (positive or negative) at the end of each month, and give an indication of when extra funds are likely to be needed

4   **Fraud detection** – There are many ways to detect that fraudulent activities may be taking place. A small organisation would not have an internal audit department but control checks can still be planned and made on a regular basis. Management should also look for staff who appear to be living a wealthier lifestyle than their position in the organisation as this may suggest that fraud is taking place. Good management, supervision and procedures in place to protect cash and assets are all good controls to prevent and detect fraud.

5   **Impact of fraud** – Fraud is effectively theft from the owners of the business. The theft can be of assets such as inventory or equipment, of cash or of time. It could be that staff are using company time to complete personal activities. Fraud reduces the profitability of the organisation and can also lead to demoralised staff; who might be aware that fraud is taking place but are afraid to report it. Fraud can also lead to a culture of mistrust which is not a very effective working environment.

Appendix 7 – Mapping Sheet

Learning Outcome	Assessment Criteria		Paragraph Numbers
1. **Demonstrate an understanding of the role of accounting within the organisation**	**1.1**	Describe the purpose, structure and organisation of the accounting function and its relationships with other functions within the organisation	**4.3** **4.4** **4.6** **5.1** **5.2** **5.3** **5.4** **Appendix 1**
	1.2	Explain the various business purposes for which the following financial information is required ■ Statement of profit or loss ■ Statement of cash flow ■ Statement of financial position (balance sheet)	**11.3.2** **11.3.3** **11.3.4** **Technical Note:** **1, 2**
	1.3	Give an overview of the organisation's business and its critical external relationships with stakeholders	**4.1** **4.2** **4.6** **5.4**
	1.4	Explain how the accounting systems are affected by the organisational structure, systems, procedures, and business transactions	**4.4** **10.1.1**
	1.5	Explain the effect on users of changes to accounting systems caused by ■ External regulations ■ Organisational policies and procedures	**5.4** **11.3.5** **11.3.11** **6.5**

Learning Outcome	Assessment Criteria	Paragraph Numbers
2. **Understand the important and use of internal control systems**	**2.1** Identify the external regulations that affect accounting practice	**4.5** **11.3.5** **11.3.11**
	2.2 Describe the causes of, and common types of, fraud and the impact of this on the organisation	**9.2** **Appendix 3**
	2.3 Explain methods that can be used to detect fraud within an accounting system	**9.1** **9.2** **Appendix 3**
	2.4 Explain the types of controls that can be put in place to ensure compliance with statutory or organisational requirements	**10.1.1** **10.1.6** **10.1.11** **10.1.13** **10.1.14** **Appendix 3**
	2.5 Explain how an internal control system can support the accounting function	**2.1** **10.1.1** **10.1.4** **10.1.8** **10.1.9** **10.1.10**
3. **Evaluate the accounting system and identify areas for improvement**	**3.1** Identify an organisation's accounting system, including hardware and software packages	**10.1** **10.1.9** **11.2.1** **10.1.5**
	3.2 Review record keeping systems to confirm whether they meet organisational requirement	**10.1.1** **10.1.4** **10.1.8** **10.1.9** **10.1.10**

Learning Outcome	Assessment Criteria	Paragraph Numbers
	3.3 Identify weaknesses in and the potential for improvements to the accounting system and consider their impact on the operation of the organisation	**Appendix 2** **6.3 eg 6.3.3** **6.4** **6.5** **9.1** **9.2**
	3.4 Identify potential areas of from arising from lack of control within the accounting system and evaluate the risk	**9.1**
	3.5 Review methods of operating for cost effectiveness, reliability and speed	**6.3**
4. Conduct an ethical evaluation of the accounting system	**4.1** Evaluate the accounting system against ethical principles	**7** **Appendix 4**
	4.2 Identify actual or possible breaches of ethics	**7** **Appendix 4**
5. Conduct a sustainability evaluation of the accounting system	**5.1** Evaluate the accounting system against sustainable principles	**8** **Appendix 5**
	5.2 Identify where improvements could be made to improve sustainability	**8** **Appendix 5**
6. Make recommendations to improve the accounting system	**6.1** Make recommendations for changes to the accounting system, including ethical and sustainability considerations with a clear rationale and an explanation of any assumptions made	**10.1**

Learning Outcome	Assessment Criteria	Paragraph Numbers
	6.2 Identify the effects that any recommended changes would have on the users of the system	**10.1.3** **10.1.5** **10.1.6** **11.2.7** **11.3.9**
	6.3 Enable individuals to understand how to use accounting systems by the use of training, manuals, information or help menus	**10.1.2** **10.1.3** **10.1.5** **10.1.6** **10.1.7** **10.1.10** **10.1.11** **10.1.13** **10.1.15**
	6.4 Identify the implications of recommended changes in terms of time, financial costs, benefits, and operating procedures	**11.2** **11.3**

INDEX

Notes

Notes

REVIEW FORM

01472   696969

Car
22

How have you used this Workbook?
(Tick one box only)

☐ Home study

☐ On a course_____

☐ Other _____

During the past six months do you recall seeing/receiving either of the following?
(Tick as many boxes as are relevant)

☐ Our advertisement in Accounting Technician

☐ Our Publishing Catalogue

Why did you decide to purchase this Workbook? *(Tick one box only)*

☐ Have used BPP Texts in the past

☐ Recommendation by friend/colleague

☐ Recommendation by a college lecturer

☐ Saw advertising

☐ Other _____

Which (if any) aspects of our advertising do you think are useful?
(Tick as many boxes as are relevant)

☐ Prices and publication dates of new editions

☐ Information on Text content

☐ Details of our free online offering

☐ None of the above

Your ratings, comments and suggestions would be appreciated on the following areas of this Workbook.

	Very useful	Useful	Not useful
Introductory section	☐	☐	☐
Quality of explanations	☑	☐	☐
Chapter tasks	☑	☐	☐
Chapter Overviews	☐	☐	☐
Index	☐	☐	☐

07904 605266

	Excellent	Good	Adequate	Poor
Overall opinion of this Workbook	☐	☐	☐	☐

Do you intend to continue using BPP Products?   ☐ Yes   ☐ No

Please note any further comments and suggestions/errors on the reverse of this page. The author of this edition can be emailed at: nisarahmed@bpp.com

Please return to: Nisar Ahmed, AAT Head of Programme, BPP Learning Media Ltd, FREEPOST, London, W12 8AA.

REVIEW FORM (continued)

TELL US WHAT YOU THINK

Please note any further comments and suggestions/errors below.